Pampered in Paris

A GUIDE TO THE BEST SPAS, SALONS AND BEAUTY BOUTIQUES

Pampered in Paris

A GUIDE TO THE BEST SPAS, SALONS AND BEAUTY BOUTIQUES

Kim Horton Levesque

Photographs by Kristyn Moore

THE LITTLE BOOKROOM

NEW YORK

Library of Congress Cataloging-in-Publication Data

Levesque, Kim Horton.
    Pampered in Paris : A Guide to the Best Spas, Salons and Beauty Boutiques /
        by Kim Horton Levesque ; photographs by Kristyn Moore.
            p. cm.
    Includes index.
    ISBN 1-892145-86-3 (alk. paper)
    1. Beauty culture–France–Paris. 2. Beauty shops–France–Paris.
        I. Moore, Kristyn. II. Title.
    TT958.5.L492 2010
    646.7'20944361--dc22
                2009040776

The following photos courtesy of: L'Espace Payot (cover, pp. 92, 93, 94-95);
Spa Anne Fontaine (inside front cover, pp. 27, 29); Spa Valmont (p. 39);
La Maison de Beauté Carita (p. 104); Maxam (p. 125, 126);
Hamman Les Cent Ciels (pp. 145, 146-47, 149); Spa Vinothérapie
Caudalie (pp. 152, 153, 154-55); U-Spa Barriere (p. 162).

Published by The Little Bookroom
435 Hudson Street, Suite 300
New York NY 10014
editorial@littlebookroom.com
www.littlebookroom.com

10 9 8 7 6 5 4 3 2 1

For Matt, Madeleine, Juliette, and Charlotte
& my parents, Roy and Donna Horton

Contents

Introduction

W here do chic and savvy Parisians go to pamper and indulge themselves? In *Pampered in Paris* I've included the best of the best—the most distinctive spas and salons, and manicure, perfume, and makeup boutiques. From the splendor of the palace hotels to the more intimate well-being centers, each place provides extraordinary service from true professionals. At these salons and spas you'll receive the best possible treatments. And perhaps equally important, the places included in this book welcome visitors from abroad whether or not they are fluent in French or familiar with European practices.

The culture of well-being and beauty thrives in Paris, not only at the *instituts* of internationally known product brands but also in the hands of individual practitioners who work in smaller, more unassuming settings. These places provide a range of services: not only traditional French treatments, but internationally inspired Thai, Chinese, and Indian therapies, as well as more modern ones like chromotherapy and ancient ones like thermal baths. In *Pampered in Paris,* you'll find a range of treatments to fit every taste and budget.

I tell you exactly what to expect at each spa—grandeur, simplicity, or something in between—and offer advice on how to navigate the cultural nuances of spa etiquette, so that anyone will feel informed and comfortable. I've also included a glossary of expressions to explain and clarify differences in French spa and salon terminology. Choosing among the services can be overwhelming, so I've provided complete descriptions and recommendations for dozens of treatments and services that are the best known, the most frequently recommended, or that are unique to an establishment. The same with products—I've singled out the ones that shouldn't be overlooked if you want to take a little bit of the French beauty experience home with you. You'll also find a list of inexpensive *pharmacie* products that are well known, highly regarded, and widely used in France.

Whether you're enveloped in the warmth of a deep-sea therapeutic bath or melting into the hands of a traditional Thai massage therapist, I hope you will find a rewarding, relaxing, and memorable glimpse into French culture. Enjoy!

—Kim Horton Levesque

THE FRENCH SPA EXPERIENCE

Etiquette & What to Expect

Spa etiquette in France is comfortably similar to that in the United States. Guests arrive between fifteen to thirty minutes before their treatment. Most spas provide a plush bathrobe, slippers, and a disposable *string*. This is a bikini bottom of varying quality, also called *un dessous*. Clients who reserve massages or body treatments are required to wear them. You will receive one from the hostess who directs you to the changing room, or from your therapist. Men must don *le string* as well. It is somewhat of a paradox that a country with such a liberal attitude towards nudity requires *strings* during a massage, but it is the protocol.

One difference women will notice in most spas and *instituts* is the scope of the body massage; it almost always includes a light chest massage. This can be relaxing for some, uncomfortable for others. The only way to know for sure if your service includes the entire body is to ask. Only one spa, Cinq Mondes, asks their clients if they are comfortable with a chest massage (*poitrine*), on a questionnaire in French and English that is filled out before a service. Simple gestures may convey your wishes, or the expression, *"Pouvez-vous éviter le massage de la poitrine, s'il vous plaît ?"* (Can you avoid massaging the chest area, please?).

Every spa selected in *Pampered in Paris* expressed an understanding of American and Asian sensitivity towards nudity. Parisian spas typically provide a sheet, blanket, or several towels for the guest to cover themselves. If you do not see a towel or sheet on the table and would like to cover up, simply ask, *"Avez-vous une grande*

serviette ou un drap?" French massage therapists do not go to the same lengths as American therapists to keep the body covered during a treatment, but even the most modest will feel quite comfortable in any of the French spas listed.

The price of the treatment almost always includes a service charge. Parisians almost never leave a gratuity, but if you are so inclined, 5% to 10% is appropriate.

The staff in luxury hotel spas and salons, or in those with international product lines, speaks adequate to exceptional English. It can be hit or miss in the boutique spas.

Spas and salons in hotels are open on Sundays, but almost all others are closed.

USEFUL TERMS

Skincare & Makeup

Base de teint / Base de maquillage :: Primer

Blush / Fard à joues :: Blush

Brillant à lèvres / Gloss :: Lip gloss

Correcteur / Anticernes :: Concealer / dark circles

Crayon à lèvres :: Lip liner

Crayon sourcils :: Eyebrow pencil

Crayon yeux :: Eyeliner pencil

Dissolvant :: Nail polish remover

Eyeliner :: Eyeliner

Fard / Ombre à paupières :: Eye shadow

Faux-cils :: False eyelashes

Fond de teint :: Foundation

Irisé :: Shimmer

Mascara :: Mascara

Pinceau :: Makeup brush

Pose de vernis / Pose vernis :: Nail polish application

Poudre :: Powder

Rouge à lèvres :: Lipstick

Vernis à ongles :: Nail polish

Spa & Institut

Soin du visage :: Facial

Soin éclat :: Skin-brightening facial

Soin anti-rides / anti-âge :: Anti-aging facial

Soins corps :: Body treatments

Modelage visage :: Facial massage

*Massage / Modelage :: Massage

Massage / Modelage raffermissant :: Firming massage

Massage / Modelage Californien ::
A light, relaxing, and fluid massage

Plus de pression / plus profonde :: Deeper pressure

Moins de pression / plus douce :: Lighter pressure

Pouvez-vous éviter le massage de la poitrine, s'il vous plaît ? ::
Can you please avoid massaging the chest area?

Évitez.....s'il vous plaît :: Avoid....please

Avez-vous une grande serviette ou un drap? ::
Do you have a large towel or sheet?

Soin amincissant :: Slimming / contouring treatment

Réflexologie plantaire :: Foot reflexology

Gommage :: Scrub / exfoliation

Enveloppement :: Body wrap

Bain :: Bath

Affusion :: Vichy shower

Épilation :: Waxing / hair removal

Épilation-maillot :: Bikini line hair removal

Teinture de cils :: Eyelash tinting

Teinture de sourcils :: Eyebrow tinting

Beauté des mains / Soin des mains :: Manicure

Manucure :: Manicure

Pose de vernis :: Nail polish application

Beauté des pieds :: Pedicure

Pédicure médicale :: Medical pedicure (use of blade)

Coupe :: Haircut

Shampooing-brushing :: Shampoo / blow dry

Mise en pli :: Hair set

Balayage :: Highlight

Soin de rasage :: Shaving treatment

*There can be confusion with the terms *modelage* and *massage* in France. A law was passed several years ago to protect physical therapists by granting them the exclusive right to use the word *massage* to describe their services. Physical therapists generally work with a medical doctor or specialist or have their own practice. They rarely work in a spa setting.

In France almost all masseuses who work in spas and salons are estheticians who have specialized massage training. Well-being centers are thus required by law to use the alternate term *modelage* instead of *massage*. Locals as well as tourists are confused by these two terms so both terms are used at spas and salons. If *massage* is used, the facility is required to provide a caveat next to it clarifying that it is a non-medical well-being treatment intended only for relaxation.

The terms are usually qualified with the following language:
La pratique du massage est le monopole des masseurs-kinésithérapeutes. Le terme "massage" est ici utilisé comme un terme générique englobant différentes techniques manuelles de modelage esthétique et de bien-être, sans visée thérapeutique. En cas de doute sur d'éventuelles contre-indications, nous vous invitons à consulter votre médecin traitant or simply, *Massage relaxant sans vertu thérapeutique.*

1st Arrondissement

L'APPARTEMENT 217

217, rue Saint-Honoré, 1st arr.
☎ 01 42 96 00 96
Métro: Tuileries
Tuesday to Saturday 10 am to 7 pm, by appointment
www.lappartement217.com (E)

The design of L'Appartement 217 embraces the principles of feng shui, and this commitment to a harmonious space is manifested in ways its guests may not even notice: insulating sheaths have been placed around equipment cables in order to neutralize electrical waves, for example; and there are crystals hidden under the wooden floors to optimize energy flow. A sense of calm pervades this chic space, enlivened by pink and

wheatgrass-green walls, colorful minimalist furnishings, and a cocktail of essential oils to purify the air. The spa is also committed to the use of top-quality natural products: the luxurious robes and linens are made from organic pine-tree pulp microfiber, and creator Stéphane Jaulin's skincare collection is formulated exclusively with organic ingredients.

Jaulin honed his skills at Kiehl's in London, as well as at Guerlain and with famed skin specialist Joëlle Ciocco in Paris, before opening L'Appartement 217 in 2005. The spa offers a short list of treatments that are personalized to meet the needs of each client. The Kiné-harmonisant massage (95€, 1 hour) uses a unique blend of therapeutic oils—selected after an evaluation of the client—to ease muscle tension, and deep pressure to help correct posture. Jaulin's signature Skin Oxygène Thérapie uses Jaulin

skincare products made with organic silicon and yam extracts to slow aging and soften wrinkles (280€, 2½ hours).

In addition to a small oxygen bar, the spa menu offers a few niche treatments, including a thirty-minute Iyashi steam treatment in which a Japanese ceramic dome is used to detox and slim the body by causing intense perspiration. Ayurvedic herbal teas are served to guests; lunch can be ordered in from, or enjoyed at, the nearby organic café Bio Boa.

✘ The hip organic eatery Bio Boa has a self-service refrigerated section as well as order-at-the-counter service. Daily specials include a Menu Detox, with choice of soup, sandwich, and fruity dessert (11€); Menu Veggie, with choice of a salad, veggie burger, and dessert (13€); and Plat Chaud, a hot selection such as grilled fish or chicken breast (14.50€). There is an excellent selection of sandwiches and salads, all between 4€ and 5€. (Bio Boa, 3, rue Danielle-Casanova, Tel. 01 42 61 17 67, Monday to Saturday 11 am to 6 pm)

LA BULLE KENZO

1, rue du Pont-Neuf, 1st arr.

✆ 01 42 36 56 73

Métro: Pont-Neuf

Monday to Saturday 11:30 am to 8 pm

www.labullekenzo.com

Ultra-hip and modern, almost futuristic in appearance, La Bulle Kenzo is a small spa on the fourth floor of the Kenzo fashion complex, just up the street from the Pont-Neuf. Designer Kenzo Takada's style—marked by color, energy, and symbols from nature—is perfectly articulated in his popular spa, where appointments for weekend massages fill up four to five months in advance.

Upon arriving at La Bulle, guests first pass through the boutique filled with perfumes and specialty *objets à sensations*, including candles, Japanese-inspired robes, and *le truc à frissons pour la tête* —a shiver-inducing object that tickles and scratches the head. The spa area is divided into two freestanding, bubble-shaped treatment rooms: La Bulle Cocoon, for calming and relaxing treatments; and La Bulle Pétillante for more invigorating services. The exterior of the first "bubble" is solid; the other is covered in what looks like plastic fur, lending texture to the monochromatic space. The interior design of the rooms reflects these contrasts —a temple-like ambience pervades the cocoon, while a suspended disco ball and soft yellow light create a hip visual sparkle in the second.

Signature treatments include the Massage aux Chandelles et au Riz, a candlelit treatment that uses rice grains and a steamed rice-scented powder for a unique sensorial experience (100€, 1 hour). The relaxing white lotus facial, Grand Soin de Lotus Blanc pour un Visage aux Anges, is one of La Bulle Kenzo's most popular options (165€, 1½ hours).

The four Kenzoki collections of skincare products for the face and body are each based on skin type and inspired by one of four natural elements: *feuille de bambou* (bamboo leaf), *fleur de gingembre* (ginger flower), *lotus blanc* (white lotus), and *vapeur de riz* (rice steam). Plant waters from these elements, extracted using a chemical-free process, form the foundation for the products. Each element carries with it unique properties for well-being: bamboo leaf is energizing; ginger flower is regenerating; white lotus is relaxing; and rice steam is soothing and nourishing.

DANIELA STEINER BEAUTY SPA /
RITZ HEALTH CLUB

In the Hôtel Ritz
15, place Vendôme, 1st arr.
☎ 01 43 16 30 60
Métro: Concorde or Tuileries
Daily 10 am to 9 pm
www.ritzparis.com (E)

The spa and health club in the iconic Ritz Hotel remains an exclusive haven that offers complete detachment from the outside world and classic Parisian luxury at its finest. The facilities are open to members and hotel guests, but a day pass (150€) may be purchased by others. The staff is welcoming and provides exceptional service. The royal treatment begins as you set foot on the red carpet that lines the steps to the entrance of this sumptuous hotel.

The Daniela Steiner Beauty Spa and Ritz Health Club is a labyrinth of countless hallways that eventually lead to a breathtaking indoor swimming pool, surrounded by frescoes and mosaics that recall the baths of ancient Greece and Rome. A domed ceiling allows natural sunlight to fill the pool space, and the pool features underwater audio and massaging jet streams for relaxation. The health club facilities include indoor squash courts, tanning beds, Jacuzzis, a *hammam* (hot steam room), saunas, and a fitness room for yoga and Pilates training and group exercise classes.

The spa and salon, decorated in a white and royal blue color scheme with natural stone floors, together seemingly offer every conceivable service from medical pedicures to waxing. A facility that caters to the world's rich and famous, the spa and salon have VIP suites and a private entrance for those hoping to pamper themselves discreetly. All guests are provided with fresh fruit, lemon water, and mint tea before and after their services. Daniela Steiner spa products are made exclusively from plant-based natural active ingredients. One massage that clients will find only at the Ritz is the Kiradjee, a therapeutic treatment based on ancestral Aboriginal techniques (200€, 90 minutes).

This center of indulgence isn't solely a woman's domain: the Ritz boasts one of the few remaining traditional barbershops in Paris. Its traditional shave is a special treat for any man (110€, 1 hour).

✗ Overlooking the Ritz's magnificent swimming pool, the Pool Bar offers cocktails, fresh fruit juices, milkshakes, and light lunches. The Mediterranean salad with feta cheese and red and yellow peppers (39€) or the platter of fresh, organic sliced fruit are two healthy offerings (25€). It is open from 11 am to 6 pm. (Ritz Health Club, 17, place Vendôme, Tel. 01 43 16 30 60)

HARNN & THANN SPA

11, rue Molière, 1st arr.

☎ 01 40 15 02 20

Métro: Pyramides

Monday to Saturday 11 am to 8 pm, Thursday until 10 pm

www.harnn.fr (E)

Stroll through a charming Parisian courtyard to enter Harnn & Thann, a boutique spa created by a Thai architect and designer. The treatments are traditional, but the space is *haute moderne*. The walls are lined with black lacquer shelves that display the broad selection of Harnn & Thann products for home and well-being, including candles, room fragrances, aromatic oils, and incense. The skincare collections are formulated with rice

bran oil and other natural ingredients. There are colorful soaps shaped like rice grains; citrus, floral, and herbal shampoos (22€); and deliciously fragrant body creams in jasmine (19€) and pomegranate (32€). The shop's bestseller is its cleansing and exfoliating black rice soap (5€), also available in versions made with red rice or white rice. The highly-regarded Harnn & Thann products are featured in a number of spas throughout the city and are also sold internationally through its website.

The Harnn & Thann Spa experience begins with a change into the appropriate clothing: for the traditional Thai massage, a loose-fitting top and bottom. Clothing is not worn for the Massage Thaï Héritage Arôma, which uses essential oils. Before clients head to their treatment rooms, they enjoy a comforting Thai footbath filled with scented water. There are five generously sized treatment rooms—including two double rooms for couples or friends—decorated with natural textures in purple and taupe. After treatments, clients are served hot tea in the spa's relaxation room. Its sky-high ceilings and abundance of natural light and greenery make it a tranquil spot to linger.

All of the therapists at Harnn & Thann attended Wat Po in Bangkok, widely regarded as the most prestigious place to study traditional Thai massage. The style combines rhythmic pressure along the body's energy lines with passive yoga-like stretches. (A video on the spa's website gives an excellent demonstration.) The effect is profoundly relaxing and therapeutic. The well-trained hands of Harnn & Thann's therapists make the massage (75€, 1 hour) memorable.

The spa menu also includes the Thai massage with essential oils; back, foot, and face massage; and the Formule Gommage du Corps, a body exfoliation that includes time in the *hammam* and uses a plant-based scrub made from sesame seeds, corn kernels, and nuts that are combined with either sugar or salt, depending on the client's skin type (95€, 1 hour).

SPA ANNE FONTAINE

370, rue Saint-Honoré, 1st arr.

✆ 01 42 61 03 70

Métro: Tuileries or Madeleine

Monday to Saturday 11 am to 8:30 pm

www.annefontaine.com (E)

T he fashion designer Anne Fontaine believes luxury and
simplicity go hand in hand. Known for the ease and elegance of her white shirts, she decided to expand into the
world of well-being in 2007. The result is an impressive urban
and organic spa located on the level below the French-Brazilian

fashion designer's boutique on rue Saint-Honoré. Anne Fontaine worked with renowned designer Andrée Putman to create the spa's breathtaking interior.

"In Brazil, white is the color of happiness," Fontaine explains; it's fitting, given Fontaine's background, that white is the pervasive color used in the spa's ultra-modern design. The décor and sometimes-austere palette are tempered, however, by the use of natural colors and textures: wood and stone, along with a waterfall that runs from the boutique through the spa, work together to bring a sense of nature inside. Fontaine's childhood in Brazil inspired her to incorporate other natural elements into the spa and her therapies; exotic fruit, essential oils and natural resins from milk are the basis for some of her treatments. Fresh rose petals scattered throughout the space add a hint of femininity.

Clients are greeted in the reception area, where they are served a cup of tea and invited to relax for a moment before being led to the dressing room. A plush robe, slippers, and a string bikini are provided. (In Paris, spas require all guests receiving body treatments to wear a *string*.) Private dressing areas are enclosed by white flowing curtains that soften the space and allow for privacy. Trays of fresh and dried fruits, water, juice, and tea are available to all guests. Miniature fresh-fruit smoothies are served post-treatment as a refreshing pick-me-up.

Anne Fontaine has an extensive treatment menu with playfully named spa packages like La Recette Anti-Déprime (Anti-Depression Recipe), La Fille d'Ipanema (The Girl from Ipanema, a body scrub, massage, and bath), and L'After Shopping (a foot bath and deep leg massage), and L'Anti-Déprimé (a scrub, massage,

and facial). The Rêve de Soie is a comforting lymphatic drainage massage that incorporates a cream made from silk fibers (195€, 1 hour 20 minutes). The Gentle Cotton Massage uses cotton oil to soothe and balance the body (145€, 50 minutes). The spa also offers facials, body wraps and scrubs, foot massage, therapeutic baths, hair removal, and nail care. Chromotherapy plays an important role in the spa and is adapted to the guest's mood and therapeutic needs. Facilities include treatment rooms for individuals and couples, Vichy showers, a Jacuzzi, and a *hammam* and sauna. This spa sets the benchmark for quality and service in Parisian spas, with talented therapists and a state-of-the art facility. Anne Fontaine plans to open her second spa in New York.

SPA NUXE

32, rue Montorgueil, 1st arr.

✆ 01 55 80 71 40

Métro: Etienne-Marcel

Monday to Friday 9 am to 9 pm, Saturday 9 am to 7:30 pm

www.nuxe.com (E)

Spa Nuxe is one of the top spa experiences available in Paris. The space is refined (and roomy, at 4800 square feet), with an East-meets-West flair. The French brand Nuxe has produced a successful line of skincare since 1957; its products are distributed in pharmacies throughout France and enjoy a massive critical and popular following. The Nuxe philosophy revolves around plant-based formulas; most of their products

are made entirely from natural materials. In 2008, Nuxe released an organic skincare line that has been incorporated into its spa services. The spa books up two months in advance for Saturdays and two to three weeks for midweek treatments. Nuxe has three other locations in Paris, but the Montorgueil location is its most impressive.

The space is stunning, with remarkably high ceilings and warm honey colors enhanced with deep red. To enter, guests walk through a pleasant courtyard and into the spa entrance where there is a space for manicures and pedicures. Adjacent to this area, the spa provides tables where clients can sample Nuxe products at their leisure before or after a service. Guests gently descend in an elevator to access the treatment rooms beneath the reception area. Spacious, comfortable rooms sit behind sliding *shoji* screen doors. Ancient arches and exposed rocks lend a medieval character to the interior, and the cool sound of running water has a soothing effect on the space.

Two of the services that have made Nuxe so popular are the Soin Aromo-lacté aux 8 Laits Vegétaux, a hydrating facial that uses eight plant milks (105€, 1¼ hours), and the profoundly relaxing Massage Sérénité, which is based on Korean and Shiatsu massage techniques (120€, 1¼ hours). Nuxe has a striking *hammam*, a lengthy menu of massages and facials, and many choices for hand and nail care. The Bain Aromatique is a therapeutic hydro-massage whirlpool bath that can be combined with facials or massages; it is filled with an infusion of plants and essential oils selected personally for each client according to the individual's mood (35€, 20 minutes). Nuxe 32 also has duo rooms and a VIP suite; it is the ultimate city escape for couples or friends.

Alternate Locations:

PRIVATE SPA NUXE HÔTEL LE MATHURIN
43, rue des Mathurins, 8th arr.
☎ 01 44 94 20 94

SPA NUXE PRINTEMPS DE LA BEAUTÉ
Printemps Haussmann
64, boulevard Haussmann, 9th arr.
☎ 01 42 82 52 52

SPA NUXE HÔTEL SQUARE
1, rue de Boulainvilliers, 16th arr.
☎ 01 46 47 24 30

SPA SAINT JAMES

In the Saint James & Albany Hotel
202, rue de Rivoli, 1st arr.
✆ 01 44 58 43 77
Métro: Louvre-Rivoli or Concorde
Daily 7:15 am to 9:15 pm
www.hotels-francepatrimoine.com/saint-james-albany/fr/
spa-paris.html (E)

Spa Saint James is keen on maintaining its reputation of exclusivity—it caters to an established clientele and relies on word-of-mouth referrals (the director explains with pride that the spa is advertised "*bouche à l'oreille*"—by word of mouth). The spa uses an entirely organic collection of massage and skincare products and offers a comprehensive menu of treatments. Spa Saint James emphasizes a holistic approach to well-being; its philosophy stresses the connection between a healthy mind and a healthy body, "*un esprit sain dans un corps sain.*"

The area for spa treatments is rather small, but behind an unassuming door, the expanse of the facility reveals itself. A luxurious swimming pool bordered by slate and bathed in ambient light provides an ideal escape from the noise and bustle outside. The pool is treated with ozone, which is used as a chemical-free alternative to harsh chlorine. The spa offers a variety of massage styles, facials, manicures, pedicures, waxing, makeup application, and fitness coaching. Guests can also arrange for a consultation with a naturopathic doctor.

Spa Saint James has one-, two-, and three-day well-being packages that combine a sampling of their services. Two niche treatments are worth discovering: the Gommage Corps Énergisant à la Pulpe de Raisins is an invigorating grape-based body exfoliation, and the Chocolate-Brown Body Sensualism envelops the body in a rich cacao cream (160€, 1½ hours). The deep-tissue massage uses warm oil and combines Swedish techniques with firm pressure to reduce stress and fatigue (130€, 1 hour).

SPA THÉMAÉ

20–22, rue Croix-des-Petits-Champs, 1st arr.
✆ 01 40 20 48 60
Metro: Palais-Royal-Musée-du-Louvre or Châtelet
Monday to Friday 11 am to 8 pm, Saturday 10 am to 8 pm
www.themae.fr (E)

Serendipity brought Guillaume Lefevre and Bertrand Thiery, the founders of Spa Thémaé, together in New York at just the right moment. Thiery, a pharmacist who had worked in the cosmetic industry for years, wanted to develop a business and well-being concept around spring water; Lefevre's focus centered on the virtues of tea. Together the two decided to create Thémaé, an urban spa that marries these two passions into a single concept.

Lefevre and Thiery spent years traveling to find the best massage therapy techniques and well-being products in the world and brought their expertise back to Paris; Thiery created all of the current nine products. Each is formulated with the 4 Teas Elixir, a blend made from pure spring water and white, black, red, and green teas. Each of these varieties serves a unique purpose: white tea has rejuvenating properties; black tea is stimulating; red tea is soothing; and green tea has antioxidants to fight aging. The amount used of each varies based on the blend's intended effects.

As clients pass through the doors of the spa, the words that inspire Thémaé are written across the wall: *Une expérience à savourer comme un thé rare venu d'une terre lointaine* ("An experience to savor like a rare tea from a distant land"). Thémaé is a Japanese word that refers to a tea-preparation ceremony, and the reception and boutique shelves display teas and tea products. Guests are also invited to sip a cup of hot tea before and after their services. With nine large treatment rooms, including one with a traditional Japanese teak bathtub, the spa seems expansive. Each room is designed with Asian minimalism in mind, accented with warm colors and black accents. The staff is fluent in English—many have lived in the U.S. and U.K.

The treatment menu is limited in order to maintain integrity and quality. It includes massages, facials, body exfoliation, and access to the *hammam*. Le Massage Singapourien is a combination of massage techniques from three cultures that targets the back, abdomen, and feet; it is ideal for those suffering from jet lag (90€, 1 hour). La Cérémonie Thémaé is a remarkable massage and facial that leaves the skin supple and refreshed (130€, 1½ hours). Thémaé was recently voted Best Urban Spa by the public during Paris's SPA-ING week.

SPA VALMONT

In the Hôtel Le Meurice
228, rue de Rivoli, 1st arr.
✆ 01 44 58 10 77
Métro: Tuileries
Daily 9 am to 8 pm
www.meuricehotel.com (E)

L e Meurice, the oldest of Paris's legendary palace hotels, is home to the Spa Valmont. The spa borders a calm, bright courtyard, which allows refreshing natural light to fill the space. It is a discreet well-being center with three treatment rooms and a lovely outdoor terrace that opens when the weather warms. The décor is elegant and refined, with white marble and rich wood accents. Celebrities such as Coco Chanel and Ingrid Bergman popularized the Valmont brand, a Swiss skincare line known for its cutting-edge formulas.

The spa menu is complete with facials, body scrubs, wraps and massage, nail care, waxing and makeup services. Valmont products are used for facials; body treatments use the marine-based collection from Les Thermes de Saint-Malo. A large Jacuzzi, mixed-gender *hammam*, fitness center, and relaxation area are available to spa guests.

Spa Valmont is known for its effective facial treatments. Le Soin Vitalité des Glaciers Régénérant is an anti-age facial that uses products made from Swiss glacial spring water and plant extracts to firm and revive the skin (200€, 1½ hours). L'Elixir des Glaciers Ultimate Treatment is a luxurious combination of an anti-aging facial and massage (395€, 2 hours 50 minutes). Spa guests can sunbathe on the terrace after or in between services, and can choose from a fairly extensive lunch menu that offers light salads, fresh fruits, and juices, as well as the house specialty: detox *macarons*.

2nd Arrondissement

AUX BAINS MONTORGUEIL

55, rue Montorgueil, 2nd arr.

✆ 01 44 88 01 78

Métro: Les Halles or Sentier

Tuesday to Sunday 10 am to 9 pm

An authentic Moroccan *hammam* that enjoys a cult following of French movie stars and international travelers, Aux Bains Montorgueil transplants the exoticism of North Africa into the heart of Paris. Owner Armand Gabbay opened the *hammam* to the public in 2004—until then, it had been his family's private retreat, where they often hosted members of Morocco's royal family who were vacationing in Paris. Its location at the end of a paved courtyard off the bustling rue Montorgueil helps

preserve its intimate ambience; Gabbay's English is impeccable, and he offers a hospitable welcome to his globe-trotting clientele.

Aux Bains Montorgueil's décor is decidedly authentic—it's all imported from Morocco. The opulence here is unmistakable: sumptuous colors and precious gold accent the spa. Just off the reception area is a relaxation room with royal blue and gold banquettes; rich, red curtains hang the length of the room. Heading down a narrow, candlelit stairway, guests enter an oasis of well-being, where vibrant pink doors open to bathrooms with golden sinks and private showers tiled in traditional blue mosaics. Traditionally, the *hammam* is divided into two or three rooms of varying temperature which become progressively hotter. In the hottest room, a hand-painted frieze of an Arabic love poem is scrolled across the wall and rose petals float in a fountain. After

twenty to thirty minutes of hot steam, the skin is ready for exfoliation. Authentic gold coins decorate the walls of the *gommage* space. A petite pool filled with cool water provides refreshment after the intense heat of the *hammam*.

The spa uses all organic products, from its black soap to the argan oil. The Rituel Marocain, which includes access to the *hammam*, exfoliation with black soap, and a one-hour massage with warm argan oil, is a good introduction to the Moroccan culture of well-being (155€). The women working here are not formally trained, but were raised in Morocco, where a visit to the *hammam* is a weekly beauty ritual for women—the tradition is handed down from generation to generation.

Guests are greeted with green tea made from fresh mint leaves, and are provided with Moroccan pastries after their services. Aux Bains Montorgueil books up well in advance, so be sure to reserve early.

BAN THAÏ SPA

5, rue Mandar, 2nd arr.

✆ 01 40 28 00 80

Métro: Sentier or Etienne-Marcel

Daily 11 am to 9 pm

www.banthaispa.fr (E)

Located in the heart of the Montorgueil pedestrian district, Ban Thaï is a center for traditional Thai massage. The Asian influence is evident as soon as guests enter the spa: an imposing Buddha fountain sits in the reception area, and the scent of jasmine permeates the space. Spa guests are greeted by their therapists with the *wai*, a traditional Thai greeting that involves a slight bow forward with the palms pressed together in a prayer

position. All of the masseuses at Ban Thaï trained at Thailand's preeminent school for Thai massage and medicine, Wat Po.

The menu of treatments is traditional, the light is low, and the ambience is relaxing. Hot tea is served as clients exchange their shoes for slippers. Guests are given a loose-fitting, pajama-like top and bottom for the Nuad Bo-rarn (traditional Thai massage, 80€, 1 hour). They head to a communal massage area where mattresses lie directly on the ground; the large massage spaces are separated with flowing curtains. For the aromatic oil massage, guests are not clothed and the treatment rooms are private (90€, 1 hour). Downstairs, there is a spacious room for couples or friends to experience a treatment together. A *hammam* is available for use, but must be reserved in advance.

Ban Thaï has eight large lounge chairs off the reception area, designed for foot massage. The Thai reflexology technique is based on an ancient Chinese method and is used to address digestive and respiratory issues as well as migraines. Therapists use a traditional wooden stick and a Thai cream—similar to Tiger Balm—made with a blend of medicinal herbs. The massage is a series of stretches and manipulations that works to stimulate lymph and blood circulation; it is a soothing escape after a long day of walking (70€, 1 hour).

3rd Arrondissement

DRAGON ET PHENIX

71, rue des Gravilliers, 3rd arr.

☎ 01 42 72 17 53

Métro: Arts-et-Métiers

Daily 1 pm to 10 pm

www.dragonetphenix.com

This area of the 3rd arrondissement is home to a large Chinese community, which has emigrated primarily from the Wenzhou region over the past few decades. This small spa, which doubles as a tea salon, seems quite at home in the neighborhood. The building has been well restored; its exposed wood beams, low ceilings, and floors planked in walnut create an intimate ambience.

The service menu is simple and includes full-body massage, along with specialized treatments for the face and feet. There are two chairs for foot massage on the ground floor and two massage rooms up a very narrow stairway. The therapists are well trained; some are Chinese students of traditional medicine on internships in Paris. In addition to massage, Dragon et Phenix offers traditional Chinese therapies like Gua Sha, a technique that uses a smooth-edged tool to gently scrape along muscles or acupuncture meridian pathways, and Er Zhu, a treatment in which special candles that produce a suctioning effect are placed into one ear at a time—the effect of both is said to be detoxifying. The rooms are clean and uncluttered.

Regular clients adore the Yu Chi facial using jade stones and essential oils (38€, 30 minutes). The gentle, yet therapeutic Tui You massage is a technique that has existed in China only for the past ten years. It seeks to balance the mind and body in an effort to relieve stress (65€, 1 hour). English speakers will feel comfortable in spite of the staff's limited English vocabulary: with choices like Massage Énergique and Massage Relaxation, the menu is mostly self-explanatory.

The tea boutique is lined with scores of gold-embossed black canisters, which contain an assortment of Chinese tea with exotic names like Garden of the Benevolent Dragon and Beijing Breeze. The owner, Li, pours cup after cup for her clients (2.50€ for a cup, 15€ for a full tasting). Dragon et Phenix hosts monthly tea tastings and initiations into the art of Chinese tea service.

INDIA & SPA
76, rue Charlot, 3rd arr.
☎ 01 42 77 82 10
Métro: Filles-du-Calvaire or République
Monday to Saturday 11 am to 9 pm, Sunday 11 am to 7 pm
www.india-spa.com

ndia & Spa is a kitschy paradise brimming with Buddha statues and treasures brought back from India and distant islands. The spa comes alive with red and orange walls, dark wood floors, and richly textured furniture and fabrics. The owner, Nathalie Amable, grew up with her grandmother in Martinique, where she learned to create drinks and elixirs from natural ingredients like cacao and local spices. She later spent time on the island of

Mauritius; Amable brought back the beauty *savoir-faire* from both regions and created India & Spa.

India & Spa's dark wood shelves are lined with the spa's own collection of products; their ingredients recall the owner's childhood and her later travels. The Huile Chocovédique is an Ayurvedic, sesame-based massage oil that hydrates the skin with a subtle scent of chocolate (26€, 200ml). A variety of nurturing shea butters in exotic scents such as cinnamon, fig, mango, and lotus flower are some of the boutique's bestsellers (29€, 200g). The receptionists and boutique staff speak English, but the therapists' language skills are more limited.

The small treatment rooms are located upstairs, with an ornately tiled *hammam* and exfoliation area downstairs. Guests are encouraged to have a hot cup of tea and relax on the cozy purple velvet couches in the relaxation room after treatments. The spa menu is lengthy with waxing and nail services, an anti-cellulite treatment, massages, facials, wraps, and scrubs. The Romance Mauricienne avec Bain de Fleurs Mixte includes a bath infused with ylang-ylang and coconut milk; a warm shea butter, vanilla, and papaya body wrap; a cucumber facial treatment; and a massage that uses warm ylang-ylang oil. This sensorial escape ends with tea and Indian pastries (140€, 2 hours).

NICKEL SPA FOR MEN

48, rue des Francs-Bourgeois, 3rd arr.

☎ 01 42 77 41 10

Métro: Saint-Paul or Rambuteau

Monday to Saturday 11 am to 7:30 pm,
Wednesday and Thursday until 9 pm

www.nickel.fr (E)

::

With four locations—two in Paris and one each in London and New York—Nickel Spa for Men sets the standard for men's luxury treatments. The main Paris location in the northern Marais is sleek, bright, and masculine. It carries more than thirty boutique skincare and perfume brands, some available exclusively in France. Clients can relax in a private lounge with large, comfy leather chairs and flat-screen TVs before their services. The treatment rooms are modern; though slightly clinical, they are well equipped with the latest in high-tech well-being equipment.

Nickel offers massages, facials, waxing, and nail services. One of the products that put Nickel on the map is the Lendemain de Fête cream (Morning-After Rescue Gel), which uses caffeine and green tea to expedite recovery after a long night on the town. The Parcours 4 day package is the perfect prescription after a tiring day in the city. It includes a facial, relaxing massage, and manicure (150€, 2½ hours).

Nickel opened the first men's salon in a department store in Paris at Printemps in the 9th arrondissement. Nickel also has a mini-spa with express services at Charles de Gaulle airport, inside the Men's Lounge boutique.

TELLEMENT ZEN

Cabinet THOTH'M

35–37, rue Beaubourg, 3rd arr.

✆ 06 15 24 07 35

Métro: Rambuteau

9 am to 8 pm, by appointment

www.tellementzen.fr

At Tellement Zen, clients will not find the accoutrements of the palace spas—and that's the point. Nor will they feel they're in what owner David Barbion calls a "factory" spa that rolls clients through. At Tellement Zen Barbion works in his own unpretentious massage space within a large apartment that he shares with practitioners of holistic medicine.

Barbion worked at the Ritz and Four Seasons Paris before leaving to practice on his own. He takes the time to get to know each person, and each guest enjoys a full-hour massage. He studied shiatsu, his specialty (50€, 1 hour), at the Ohashi Institute; he also offers massages with essential oils (70€, 1 hour). Clients don't have to travel to the apartment to take advantage of his services—he will make house calls to homes and hotels for massage (25€ travel fee). But Tellement Zen is worth a visit: the space is filled with natural light and soothing colors; a king-sized mattress rests on the floor. Barbion's style is intuitive and precise, his movements seamless.

Before a client leaves, David presents him or her with a red box. Inside are small pieces of folded paper that contain wishes for happiness and positive energy. It is a sincere and gentle gesture that inspires clients to take a little bit of the Zen spirit to the world outside.

4th Arrondissement

LES BAINS DU MARAIS

31–33, rue des Blancs Manteaux, 4th arr.

☎ 01 44 61 02 02

Métro: Rambuteau or Hôtel de Ville

Monday, Friday, and Saturday 10 am to 8 pm;

Tuesday, Wednesday, Thursday, and Sunday 10 am to 11 pm

www.lesbainsdumarais.com

A taste of North Africa greets you at the door of Les Bains du Marais, with two Moroccan lanterns flanking an enormous, dark brown coach door. The spa is decorated in warm colors—oversized dark brown tiles, deep walnut floors, and flowing cream-colored curtains. A step inside is a clean break with the outside world.

Les Bains is a full-service spa and salon with a comprehensive spa menu and on-site restaurant. The spa has a large *hammam* with two rooms of progressive heat, treatment rooms for facials and massages, a relaxation area, and an adjacent salon for hair and nail services. It is easy to spend a full day at Les Bains du Marais: in fact, to experience it fully, you will need that long.

Les Bains has one of the most pleasing *hammams* in central Paris. It is split into two areas and it is roomy, but steam and low light preserve privacy. The first area has several banquettes long enough for reclining, along with two showers to cool off after the heat. The hotter room is smaller, but still offers plenty of room to lounge. It is open only to women on Mondays, Tuesdays, and Wednesdays, and reserved for men on Thursdays and Fridays. On Wednesday evenings, Saturdays, and Sundays, the *hammam* is mixed and swimsuits are required.

The *hammam* ritual does not end after the steam rooms. If you reserve a *gommage* (scrub) treatment, you will be called by name and directed to the exfoliation area. Your skin will be clean and baby-soft after the humid heat of the *hammam* and a vigorous twenty-minute scrub by the therapists. Access to the sauna and *hammam*, along with an exfoliation treatment, lasts two hours; a robe, slippers, and an exfoliation glove are provided (70€, 2 hours). The Journée Beauté et Soin du Corps includes sauna and *hammam* access, exfoliation, and a relaxing massage with essential oils (130€, 3 hours).

The tea salon and restaurant serves light but generously portioned salads (12€–21€), sandwiches (11€–15€), pastas, and desserts. Well-cushioned benches and light colors create a comforting ambience. Guests are invited to linger restfully with a cup of hot tea and keep activity light after the *hammam* ritual. Be advised: the spa is busy on the weekends. Weekdays are quieter, and the spa is easily accessible.

SHIATSU JEAN-MARC WEILL
56-58-60, rue Saint-Antoine, 4th arr.
☎ 01 48 04 94 02
Métro: Saint-Paul
By appointment
www.shiatsu-weill.com

I f you are looking for a masterful, no-frills shiatsu experience, Jean-Marc Weill is the ideal practitioner. Weill lived in New York for three years and trained at the Ohashi Institute with one of the world's few Shiatsu Master Practitioners. He takes a holistic approach to health and, for this reason, studied subjects that complemented his massage practice: he trained in traditional Chinese medicine for three years, with one year of specialization in Chinese nutrition. He is also a certified Master of Sophrology, a series of therapeutic mental and physical exercises that work to reduce stress. Sophrology is partially subsidized by the French health-care system for patients with certain conditions. Weill works with natural practitioners in adjacent apartments to provide well-rounded solutions for his clients.

The space is simple; there is a tiny reception area with three chairs and a table. The massage room is unremarkable, with a large futon-like mattress that occupies the entire room. To best assess clients' needs, Weill listens—to their requests and explanations, yes, but more importantly to their tone of voice. He also observes their movements and notices any scents they might exude. He prefers to talk about measured penetration rather than pressure when it comes to massage. Weill specializes in massaging pregnant women and those with chronic pain. The menu is straightforward: 60€ for a one-hour massage or five sessions for 275€.

5th Arrondissement

RASA YOGA

21, rue Saint-Jacques, 5th arr.

☎ 01 43 54 14 59

Métro: Cluny-la-Sorbonne

Daily for yoga classes; spa services available by appointment

www.rasa-yogarivegauche.com (E)

The rue Saint-Jacques in the Latin Quarter is often loud and frenetic, but to step through the enormous doors and into the courtyard at Rasa Yoga is to enter a serene haven. Five years ago, Daniela Schmid realized her dream of owning a holistic sanctuary, dedicated to yoga and well-being, right in the heart of Paris. In Sanskrit, *rasa* means "the best of everything, the nectar," and the facilities offer a sampling of the best in holistic

7.00 – 9.00 mysore
10.00 –11.30 ashtanga
13.00 –14.30 iyengar
15.00 –16.30 intégral
17.00 –18.30 vinyasa
18.30 –20.00 alignement
20.00 –21.30 ashtanga

samedi 23 mai

10.00 –12.00
12.00 –12.00

health care and prevention including a yoga studio with daily classes, treatment rooms for holistic therapies, a tea and fresh-fruit juice bar, and a boutique. The staff is international and multilingual, but most yoga classes are taught in French. Rasa Yoga was, in 2007, named one of the top 25 yoga studios in the world in *Travel & Leisure*.

Rasa is a light, minimalist space where people feel immediately relaxed and nurtured; neutral colors and natural textures dominate. Rasa offers Ayurvedic, shiatsu, Thai, and other specialty massages. Exclusive to Rasa is the Massage Esalen, a technique developed in California that combines Swedish massage with gentle rocking, stretching, acupressure, and aromatherapy (90€, 1¼ hours). Other well-being therapies include reflexology and reiki energy-balancing sessions. There is also a well-established series of workshops for expectant mothers and new parents. The sessions include pre- and post-natal massage for mothers (80€, 1 hour) and sessions where parents learn to massage their infants (50€, 30 minutes).

6th Arrondissement

BOUTIQUE BOUDOIR ANNICK GOUTAL

12, place Saint-Sulpice, 6th arr.

✆ 01 46 33 03 15

Métro: Saint-Sulpice

Monday to Saturday 10 am to 7 pm

www.annickgoutal.com (E)

Annick Goutal was first known as a legendary Parisian perfumer—she created twenty-eight fragrances in all, nineteen for women and nine for men. French President François Mitterrand's preferred cologne, Eau d'Hadrien, established Goutal's reputation: it is a citrus scent made with Italian lemons, grapefruits, and a hint of cypress. The three spas or "boutique boudoirs" created by Goutal, ultra-feminine havens of relaxation, have been incorporated into her perfume boutiques. Since 1999, Annick's daughter Camille Goutal has directed and expanded the Annick Goutal brand.

The boudoirs are decorated in soft colors: pink, champagne, and rose. The boudoir on rue Castiglione is draped in silky fabrics, with Baccarat chandeliers hanging overhead and soft classical music playing in the background.

Treatments are based on Goutal's Damascus Rose skincare collection; they are tailor-made for each client by combining an active rose serum with essential oils and vegetable extracts. The whimsically named treatments, most of them referencing famous women in French history, have garnered a lot of positive attention and created a loyal following in the beauty and fashion world. The Marie Antoinette is a massage that uses a personalized mixture of essential oils, including rose oil, thyme, rosemary, and lavender—

the concoction is based on the client's mood (150€, 1½ hours). The Aliénor d'Aquitaine is an express, deep-pressure anti-jetlag massage that targets the shoulders, back, and neck with essential oils (50€, 30 minutes). The boudoirs offer facials, massages, manicures and pedicures; a traditional rose and shea butter wax is used for hair removal. The spa also features seasonal treatments that change with the weather.

Alternate Locations:

14, rue de Castiglione, 1st arr.
✆ 01 42 60 52 82

3 bis, rue des Rosiers, 4th arr.
✆ 01 48 87 80 11

16, rue de Bellechasse, 7th arr.
✆ 01 45 51 36 13

93, rue de Courcelles, 17th arr.
✆ 01 46 22 00 11

GALERIE CLARIDGE
74, avenue des Champs Elysées, 8th arr.
✆ 01 45 63 33 38

INSTITUT SAARA

10, rue Christine, 6th arr.
✆ 01 46 33 31 50
Métro: Odéon
Open Monday and Saturday 10 am to 7 pm,
Tuesday to Friday 9 am to 8 pm
www.institutsaara.fr (E)

:::

nstitut Saara offers three conveniently located spas in the 6th arrondissement. The colors are light and natural, and the ambience is made charming by ancient arches and exposed beams. The rue Christine location is the best appointed of the three; the smaller spa on rue Bourbon le Château is pleasant, but has a more clinical atmosphere.

The expansive spa menu offers everything from jet lag and chocolate massages to slimming treatments to Power Plate coaching sessions, yet the quality remains remarkably consistent even given this wide variety of services. Institut Saara is known for le Soin Aquasvelt and Soin Liposvelt, two treatments said to target cellulite with remarkable efficiency. The esthetician determines the client's type of cellulite, chooses the appropriate serum, and then applies it with a deep massage. The treatment is done by hand without any equipment; an appropriately warm or cold body wrap follows (60€, 45 minutes). The Shine Harmony Massage is a Tibetan-style full-body massage that uses dried herbs individually selected for clients. The herbs are placed into a pouch, heated, and applied to the body; the massage works along acupressure meridians to soothe and tone (90€, 1½ hours). The spa also has a salon for hair and nail care and offers permanent makeup services.

Alternate Locations:

3, rue de Bourbon Le Château, 6th arr.
☏ 01 55 42 61 50

5, rue de Médicis, 6th arr.
☏ 01 43 54 06 03

17, rue de Laos, 15th arr.
☏ 01 40 65 97 74

125, rue de la Pompe, 16th arr.
☏ 01 47 27 44 72

SIX AND SPA BY IDA DELAM

In Hôtel le Six
14, rue Stanislas, 6th arr.
✆ 01 42 22 62 67
Métro: Vavin
Monday to Saturday 11 am to 8 pm, Sunday 1 pm to 6 pm
www.idadelam.com

Ida Delam's journey into the world of well-being began on a trip to Oman, where the synchronicity of an idea, a place, and a perfume all came together for this enthusiast of ancient culture. Upon her return to France, she was prepared to follow her heart's path and created a proprietary blend of oils, l'Huile Secrète, or Secret Oil, which forms the basis of her skincare collection.

Six and Spa is tucked into a quiet part of the 6th arrondissement, in a smart and unassuming boutique hotel, which hosts primarily British and French businessmen. The design is sleek and contemporary, with concrete floors, neat lines, and red accents. Downstairs, the spa is softly lit, with rich colors and intimate treatment spaces.

Delam discovered massage at the age of ten in the *hammam* she frequented with her grandmother. After formal training, she created her own signature massage style, the Modelage Omanais. The Soin Grain de Folie is a soft, subtle combination of massage and exfoliation. The texture of the sand is selected according to the guest's skin type; it comes from Mauritius, Seychelles, Hawaii, Corsica,

and Havana (115€, 1 hour). Le Soin Omanais uses large granules of sugarcane to exfoliate the body. After the skin is velvety soft, Delam warms her Huile Secrète for a gentle massage (125€, 1 hour). The spa menu includes massages, facials, and exfoliation treatments. The *hammam* is covered in pearly-white mosaic tiles with a starry ceiling overhead, and is available to complement services.

Ida Delam wanted the spa experience to be integrative; she created a candle to perfume the space and produced a soundtrack called *Ambiance Spa*. Her latest venture is a perfume, "le 6," released in September 2010. Her products are sold exclusively at the Ritz Paris and in her own spa.

SPA L'OCCITANE

47, rue de Sèvres, 6th arr.

☎ 01 42 22 88 62

Métro: Sèvres-Babylone

Monday to Saturday 9:30 am to 7:30 pm, Thursday until 9 pm

www.loccitane.fr (E)

O ne of the trendsetters in French natural cosmetics, l'Occitane opened its first Parisian spa in December 2008, just across from Le Bon Marché department store in the 6th arrondissement. The spa is imbued with the atmosphere of the Camargue region in southern France, the location of l'Occitane's flagship spa. Guests enter through a boutique, where a huge selection of l'Occitane products are displayed.

The shapes and colors of Provence inspire l'Occitane's décor. The sand-colored walls, hues of golden honey, and natural light create a refreshing and open space. In the relaxation area, guests are invited to taste hot tea, dried figs, and plums. Natural materials are abundant: bamboo, stone, and woven textures adorn five spacious rooms that are accessible to those with limited mobility.

One of the spa's most popular treatments is the Secret de lumière à l'Immortelle. This facial uses a Vitamin C-enriched formula to smooth and brighten skin affected by the sun or age spots (80€, 1 hour). Facials and massages can be combined with therapeutic and relaxing baths that integrate natural components like lavender, grapes, and vervain (35€, 25 minutes). In addition to massage, baths, and facials, the spa offers treatments for legs, stomach, back, and hands; body wraps and scrubs; and waxing services. The staff is helpful, and most speak English.

Luxury meets ecological sensitivity in this well-being space: the spa goes to great lengths to conserve water, and its linens are made from organic cotton grown on environmentally-conscious farms that do not use pesticides or fertilizer. Spa l'Occitane has created a tranquil and refined ambience, one that is particularly suited to American spa sensibilities.

LES THERMES SAINT-GERMAIN
5, passage de la Petite-Boucherie, 6th arr.
☎ 01 56 81 31 11
Métro: Saint-Germain-des-Prés
Monday to Saturday 10 am to 8 pm, Thursday until 11 pm;
Sunday 2 pm to 9 pm
www.les-thermes.com

A charming spa on a quiet street near the Buci market area, Les Thermes Saint-Germain offers unique services to a largely neighborhood clientele. Soothing marine colors and blue mosaic tiles lend a Mediterranean touch to the setting. A small boutique sells products used in Les Thermes' services— Carita for facials, Thalgo for body treatments, and Rose & Pepper, an all-natural line for both types of treatments. The spa offers a lengthy list of massages—some with an exotic flair—along with waxing, tanning and nail services.

Les Thermes is located in an ancient building that has been restored with care. Guests descend a narrow stairway to the treatment area, where vaulted ceilings expand an otherwise small space. There is a private *hammam* and an exfoliation area for *gommage* services. The two-hour Cure Orientale package allows access to the *hammam*, followed by *gommage*, a Rassoul application, and a thirty-minute Massage Oriental (122€). Rassoul (or Rhassoul) is a Moroccan clay that has been used as a soap, shampoo, and skin conditioner for more than fourteen hundred years. Its absorption properties make it popular in skin conditioning and detoxification treatments.

The Buci area that borders the spa is filled with some of the finest chocolate shops in Paris—Pierre Marcolini, Patrick Roger, and Pierre Hermé—but if eating chocolate doesn't satisfy your craving, you can be slathered in it at Les Thermes. The energizing Massage Chocolat uses a cacao exfoliation followed by a massage with cacao oil (85€, 1 hour). Cacao is a natural ingredient with anti-oxidant properties often used in regenerative anti-aging treatments. Some of the spa's more novel services include a bamboo massage, Massage aux Bambous, and Coconut's Dream, a body therapy that uses the entire coconut: its milk, meat, and pulp to nourish, and its shell to apply pressure during the massage (100€, 1 hour).

7th Arrondissement

INSTITUT DARPHIN

97, rue du Bac, 7th arr.

✆ 01 45 48 30 30

Métro: Rue du Bac

Monday through Wednesday 11 am to 7 pm, Thursday 11 am to
9 pm, Friday 10 am to 8 pm, Saturday 10 am to 7 pm

www.darphin.fr

In 1958, Pierre Darphin opened one of the first *instituts* (salons) in Paris, with a new concept: Institut Darphin went beyond hairdressing to address body and skincare issues. Darphin believed that a woman's skin was a visible "screen" upon which her lifestyle, environment, and choices in beauty care were projected. At the core of his philosophy were treatments personalized to each client. His salon catered to Europe's most famous and fashionable women of the time.

Today, the reception and treatment rooms in both salons are white and bright. In Paris, the majority of spas are located in cellars of ancient buildings, where, despite state-of-the-art lighting, the atmosphere may be a bit subdued, but the soaring space here is flooded with natural light. The space in the 7th arrondissement is petite, with three treatment rooms; the Saint-Honoré spa is much larger, with five. The salon on rue Saint-Honoré is housed in the mansion where Napoleon celebrated his marriage to Josephine de Beauharnais, in 1796.

The *institut* is known for its luxurious beds and armchairs, the contours of which help circulation and which recline to various positions. After an in-depth interview, a Darphin therapist chooses the color of the treatment room (see Chromotherapy, page 174), ambient music, and aromatic oils to suit the guest's needs. The idea is that this personalized care will optimize the client's sense of well-being and enhance the overall experience.

Darphin's contemporary philosophy is known as "3D Skincare." The protocol includes Darphin Serums that target specific issues; Aromatic Care, during which aromatic essential oils are inhaled before being applied to the skin; and, finally, skin cream. Aromatherapy is one of the most unique aspects of the skincare line: Pierre Darphin appreciated the value of a multisensory experience in well-being treatments. He believed the sense of smell was the most significant factor that could have a positive, transformational effect, as it evoked a "sensation of pleasure."

The *institut* offers a long list of massages, specialized facials, exfoliation and slimming body treatments, manicures, pedicures, and waxing services. Color tinting for eyebrows and eyelashes is available, as is hair bleaching for face and arms. Darphin's signature treatment is the Soin Divin Jeunesse aux 8 Fleurs, the Divine 8 Flower Lifting Facial (190€, 1¾ hours). It is an anti-aging treatment designed to tone, tighten and lift. The Soin Booster d'Éclat à l'Iris et au Mimosa is a facial that treats dull skin in need of a brightening boost (100€, 1 hour). Institut Darphin has created a special menu of services for men, as well, which includes a deep-cleansing facial using lemon and menthol, an anti-age treatment with gingko-biloba, and a relaxing, anti-stress therapy with cucumber and lavender (all 100€, 1 hour).

Alternate Location:

350, rue Saint-Honoré, 1st arr.

✆ 01 47 03 17 70

SENSATION SPA
8, villa de Saxe, 7th arr.
☎ 01 47 34 26 19
Métro: Ségur or Ecole-Militaire
Monday through Saturday 10 am to 8 pm
www.sensation-spa.com

Located between the Eiffel Tower and Montparnasse, Frederic Bonfils and his team have created a peaceful retreat in Sensation Spa. The exterior is unremarkable—it looks like a brick apartment building on a quiet cul-de-sac—but entering the building reveals a calming sanctuary where a truly talented masseur and his team work to heal and nurture. Before massaging professionally, Bonfils traveled the world in search of the best mas-

sage techniques and began massaging by intuition. After realizing that he was offering treatments to dozens of friends and associates each week, he knew he had found his calling. Now Bonfils trains, at his own school, more than eight hundred students per year for Sothys, Hotel Park Hyatt Paris-Vendôme, and other highly regarded spas.

The space is a Zen haven. Statues of Buddha, river rocks, bamboo, and other artifacts from Bonfils's stays in Asia nestle in discreetly amidst neutral colors. The treatment room that faces the Japanese garden is especially tranquil, as it allows natural light into the space. For a taste of the Tao, the Massage Tibétain aux Bols Chantant is a nurturing and balancing experience. The music of the Tibetan bowls is said to stimulate inward reflection and promote relaxation (90€, 1 hour). The signature treatment at Sensation Spa is the

Massage Créatif, which combines the gentle motion of a California massage with the toning effect of the Swedish technique. Bonfils's unique style also includes elements of shiatsu and reflexology. The combination is unorthodox, but the result is intuitive, very personal, and built on classic fundamentals (85€, 1 hour or 110€, 1½ hours). Sensation Spa offers facials, body wraps, and treatments under a Vichy shower. A small *hammam* is also available for up to six people.

Bonfils's spa reflects his cosmopolitan sensibilities; he speaks English and is particularly sensitive to the American and Asian sense of modesty.

8th Arrondissement

ANNE SÉMONIN SPA
In Le Bristol Hotel
112, rue du Faubourg Saint-Honoré, 8th arr.
✆ 01 42 66 24 22
Métro: Miromesnil or Saint-Phillipe-du-Roule
Monday to Saturday 11 am to 8 pm
www.lebristolparis.com (E)

The Anne Sémonin Spa is one of Paris's most luxurious get-aways. There are two entrances to the spa: an interior passage connects it with the hotel, and the second opens directly onto rue du Faubourg Saint-Honoré. If you have time, take the former route: a walk through Le Bristol reveals Parisian elegance at its best. Marble floors and columns, brilliant natural light, crystal chandeliers, sumptuous red area rugs, dashes of pomegranate, and heavy crimson tapestry curtains decorate the lounge and reception area. Fresh flowers bring life to the space. By contrast, the spa is contemporary and minimalistic, with café-au-lait walls and taupe stone floors; the Anne Sémonin Spa has been a part of Le Bristol for fifteen years, but was remodeled two years ago. The design is simple and efficient; everything from preparation to relaxation takes place inside one of the treatment rooms. A large treatment room is available for a mother-daughter, girlfriend, or couple retreat. The therapists work with international clients daily, and the spa menu and website are available in English.

At the outset of a client's appointment, the esthetician escorts the guest to a softly lit room; the eye is drawn to a table where sparkling bottles filled with essential oils are meticulously arranged. After a thorough examination of the skin and a short interview, the therapist mixes an elixir of active plant serums and essential oils to suit the client's immediate skincare concerns. The spa has made its name with its signature detoxifying and brightening facial, L'Expérience Anne Sémonin. An ozone tool provides a targeted treatment that helps bring out sub-surface blemishes. Spa director and beauty therapist Celine Helmstetter has magical hands. Her care is thorough and intuitive, and the final result is remarkable: a visible difference in your skin (115€, 55 minutes). As the guests find their bearings at the end of the service, a small pick-me-up tray of goodies is brought in, with juice, tea, or water and a sampling of delectable *macarons*.

The spa menu includes facials, massages, specialized eye therapy,

body wraps, anti-cellulite treatments, and nail care; a separate selection of facials caters especially to men's needs. The Soin Anti-Rides 100% Actif Masculin is a tightening and lifting facial that uses Anne Sémonin's cryotherapeutic Express Radiance Ice Cubes, to brighten skin (115€, 55 minutes). TJ's, a bustling full-service hair and nail salon, is located immediately next to the spa within the hotel and can fulfill any additional beauty requests.

✗ Le Bar du Bristol is a bar-lounge also located in Le Bristol. The Anne Sémonin Spa does not order in for clients, but Le Bar is so close and sumptuous that it deserves a peek. The ravioli with lobster in a butter, basil, and citrus sauce is indulgent (45€). For something on the lighter side, try the Caprese salad (29€).

ESPACE FRANCE ASIE

11, rue du Chevalier-de-Saint-George, 8th arr.
☎ 01 49 26 08 88
Métro: Madeleine or Concorde
Monday to Saturday 10:30 am to 8 pm
www.espace-france-asie.com

Miki Suwanachoti, founder of Espace France Asie, was a driving force in overcoming stereotypes about Thai massage and promoting the traditional method in Paris. Many Parisians associated Thai massage with erotic massage. Suwanachoti, who trained in Bangkok under Master Ting at Temple Wat Po, opened her spa in 1992 and organized informational sessions to overcome this misconception and to demonstrate tradi-

tional Thai methods. She quickly established a clientele. In 1997 she opened The Miki School; she now teaches hundreds of masseuses each year. The interior of Espace France Asie was imported almost entirely from Thailand, including wooden facades and shutters of traditional Thai houses that now cover the exterior of the treatment rooms. One of the most striking elements of the décor is the wall covered in thousands of miniature Buddha tiles from Suwanachoti's personal collection. There is an enormous Buddha statue and altar in the reception area. A smaller image of Buddha's personal doctor, Dr. Shivago Komarpaj, to whom the origins of Thai massage are attributed, sits at his side.

After changing into the loose-fitting clothes typical of Thai massage, guests are welcomed with a cup of hot tea. The massage rooms are private (those to the right of the reception area are filled with more sunlight than those along the hallway).

The treatment menu at Espace France Asie is simple: Nuad Bo-rarn, traditional Thai massage (80€, 1 hour); pedicure with foot massage (80€, 70 minutes); a massage with sesame oil; facials; and a fantastic day package, the Formule Wanalaï. The Formule includes a Thai massage, Thai foot bath, one-hour foot reflexology massage, and a thirty-minute back massage with cream (200€, 3 hours). The goal of the therapy is to bring balance to the function of the four basic elements in the body: earth (bones and muscles), water (blood and secretions), fire (digestion and metabolism), and air (breathing and blood circulation). Suwanachoti says she and her staff keep their thoughts positive to promote healing energy as they treat clients.

The therapists' technique at France Asie is profound and effective. The language barrier is not usually an issue in traditional Thai massage spaces in Paris—most masseuses speak limited French themselves, but are nonetheless exceptionally adept at spotting the client's trouble spots. Facial expressions combined with pointing make for efficient communication.

ESPACE JOÏYA

6, rue de la Renaissance, 8th arr.

✆ 01 40 70 16 49

Métro: George V or Alma-Marceau

Monday to Wednesday and Saturday 11 am to 7:30 pm,
Tuesday and Thursday 11 am to 9 pm

www.joiya.fr

::

The best in Russian and Asian well-being techniques have come together in this Parisian space. The spa's founder, Julia Lemigova, was the last Miss USSR in 1991 and second runner-up in the Miss Universe pageant that same year; she left bathing suits and ball gowns far behind, and today owns and manages Espace Joïya. Recently, she launched her own 100%-natural skincare line, called Russie Blanche. The formulas are based on Russian medicinal plants and traditional herbal recipes.

The spa was completely renovated in 2009. Neutral tones, earthy textures, and an Asian motif decorate the center. The skincare collection sits pretty in crisp black and white packaging on the boutique's shelves. Espace Joïya offers traditional Asian massages, facials, therapeutic body wraps, manicures, pedicures, and slimming and firming treatments. The Massage Russie Blanche is a therapeutic and energizing massage that blends Thai and Russian massage techniques with aromatherapy (130€, 1½ hours). The Réflexologie Plantaire is a deep-pressure therapy that works the acupressure points of the feet to balance the body's energy (95€, 1 hour).

L'ESPACE PAYOT

62, rue Pierre-Charron, 8th arr.

☎ 01 45 61 42 08

Métro: Franklin-D.-Roosevelt

Monday to Friday 7 am to 10 pm, Saturday 9 am to 7 pm,
Sunday 10 am to 5 pm

www.espacepayot.fr

"For the longest time I took care of my body—until the day I realized that I needed to take care of my soul," said Dr. Nadia Payot. These words (spoken more than eighty years ago) remain the guiding philosophy of L'Espace Payot, a spa and fitness club based on the techniques and products of Dr. Payot—one of the first female licensed medical doctors in

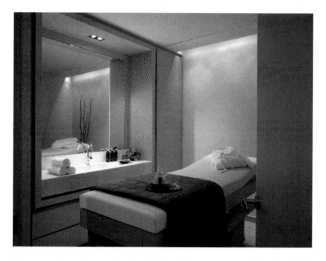

France and a pioneer in the field of beauty and well-being. The design is modern, the facility is state-of-the-art, and the space is roomy at 13,000 square feet. L'Espace Payot is located just off of the Champs-Elysées.

The spa is known for its facials, which use the forty-two-movement sculpting method created by Dr. Payot. The technique is a series of manual treatments designed to increase circulation, thereby regenerating and rejuvenating the skin. Le Soin Energétique Minéral à la Poudre de Diamante, or Energetic Mineral Facial with Diamond Powder, is a therapy that manually sculpts the face and uses products made with diamond powder and semi-precious stones (230€, 2 hours).

L'Espace Payot is equipped with a grand swimming pool, sauna,

hammam, Jacuzzi, and gym. The gym offers courses in Pilates, aquatic gymnastics, yoga, and Power Plate, as well as private training. The therapy rooms are roomy and equipped with chromotherapy technology; the floors are heated, and each room has a private shower. After consulting with the client, the therapist will select light, color, and music to complement the treatment. In addition to the typical spa services, guests can make reservations for wax-

ing and tanning, manicures, pedicures; enjoy Vichy shower treatments or therapeutic baths; and consult with nutritional advisors or Reiki practitioners. Clients who reserve a spa service have access to the *hammam* and sauna. For access to the pool and gym, they must purchase a separate day pass. Payot also offers memberships, which include full access to the facilities seven days a week (2400€, 6-month membership).

ESPACE WELEDA

10, avenue Franklin-D.-Roosevelt, 8th arr.

☎ 01 53 96 06 15

Métro: Franklin-D.-Roosevelt or Saint-Phillipe-du-Roule

Tuesday to Friday 10:30 am to 7 pm, Saturday 2 pm to 7 pm

www.espace-weleda.fr

Weleda, one of the most established names in natural skincare and well-being products, has created a colorful spa just a few blocks from the Champs-Elysées. The company, named after the Celtic goddess of wisdom and healing, has produced organic products since 1921. Designers brought nature inside the spa, with a wall of vegetation in the reception area that flows with the soothing sound of water. A boutique shares

the space, with modern shelves showcasing the company's products. Like Weleda's packaging, the space is bright and full of life. The facility is multi-functional, offering fitness training as well as workshops that range from therapeutic self-massage to baby massage for new parents.

Modern lines and vibrant color make Espace Weleda a cheerful place. The three treatment rooms are clean and simple, with light birch wood and a pleasing scent. Guests first choose an oil for their massages—lavender, rose, or arnica—and then the therapist selects the appropriately colored treatment room. The menu is limited to massages and facials. The Massage Vitalité aux Fruits is an energizing therapy that stimulates the senses with a citrus-scented oil or Sea Buckthorn oil, depending on the skin's condition (95€, 1¼ hours). The spa is also known for its Modelage Jeunesse et Fermeté, a gentle anti-aging facial that uses Weleda's Wild Rose product line to soothe skin (65€, 45 minutes). Weleda's products are widely available in the United States; this Swiss brand has also opened a spa in New York's Hudson Valley.

In the Hôtel Plaza Athénée
25, avenue Montaigne, 8th arr.
✆ 01 53 67 65 66 3565
Métro: Franklin-D.-Roosevelt
Daily 8 am to 10 pm
www.plaza-athenee-paris.fr/fitness_spa/index.html (E)

Walking into the Institut Dior is like sitting front row at an *haute couture* show in Paris: as they wind around the staircase that leads into the spa, guests are entranced by a giant video screen projecting a Christian Dior runway show. Here, Dior has created spa *haute couture*.

The Hôtel Plaza Athénée has enjoyed a long relationship with Christian Dior. He moved his studio to the avenue Montaigne in 1946, just up the street from the Plaza. The hotel became a source of inspiration for him; he named several designs after it—the Plaza and the Athénée suits. It became the place where Dior entertained and dined with the world's fashionable and famous; it also became a refuge where he could steal away into a private lounge for a moment alone.

Today, the *institut* glows in radiant white. Once a guest is inside the spa, his or her eye is drawn to an impressive water-filled basin with a scrolled mosaic design, above which a glass droplet is suspended. The service is impeccable; within seconds, a hostess appears to offer a plate of fresh fruit and water, tea, or other drink. Lounge chairs are long, white, and luxurious. Photos of Dior models in front of the Plaza, along with sketches of Dior's designs, decorate the hallway that leads to the treatment rooms.

The spacious treatment rooms are crisp white with soft, gray accents; the silver and white CD monogram is emblazoned on the walls. A gray, tiered ceiling dotted with tiny lights floats over the stunning VIP room, where the esthetician consults with the client over an elegant marble table. The Institut Dior philosophy centers on reactivating youthfulness; the Dior Salon has an exclusive, high-tech micro-abrasion technique for the body and face that uses exfoliation, photo-stimulation and lymph-draining to revitalize the skin. A *hammam* and sauna are available to use pre- and post-treatment. Guests receive a *petite remise*, a makeup reapplication from an esthetician, as part of their service.

The *institut* offers manicures, pedicures, massage, specialized facials, and targeted body treatments, and includes services especially for men. Three- to five-day programs are available, as are two-week series of anti-aging and regenerating therapies. A ninety-minute bust and *décolleté* firmness treatment, as well as the Contre-Attaque Cellulite, which targets the area from the waist to the thighs, are both part of the Youthfulness body series (240€ each). Near the entrance to the hotel, an elegant lounge and café surrounds the building's light- and foliage-filled interior courtyard. It resonates with the calming sound of a harp player and has a few healthy selections for a spa lunch.

INSTITUT MARC DELACRE

17, avenue George V, 8th arr.

✆ 01 40 70 99 70

Métro: Alma-Marceau

Monday 11 am to 7 pm, Tuesday to Thursday 10 am to 7 pm,
Friday and Saturday 10 am to 6:30 pm

www.marcdelacre.com (E)

Parisian businessmen and politicians were instantly seduced by the concept of a salon and spa devoted to well-being and beauty services for men: they no longer had to subject themselves to the awkward and curious stares that can come from a primarily female clientele. Institut Marc Delacre, created by one of the most famous hairdressers in Paris, opened in 1990 and has been a hit ever since. Most of the staff speaks English and deals daily with an international clientele, and Marc Delacre's website makes the salon easily accessible.

The space is reminiscent of a private men's club, with golden-brown sycamore wood, marble floors, and steel accents. The salon is spacious, with fourteen black leather armchairs and secluded hairdressing stations for added privacy. Hairdressers are skilled in styles from the classic to the cutting-edge. Marc Delacre is one of the few salons to offer an old-fashioned wet shave; warm towels scented with eucalyptus oil, a soothing almond-oil massage, and an old-style shave make this a memorable indulgence (39€, 30 minutes).

Manicures, pedicures, massage, exfoliation treatments, facials, waxing, tanning, scalp and foot massages are featured on Marc Delacre's menu. A sauna, *hammam*, restaurant, and relaxation room augment the pampering experience. Le Soin du Visage 1ère Classe is a deep-

cleansing facial that works to stimulate lymph drainage and promote better skin circulation for more toned skin (163€, 1 hour
25 minutes).

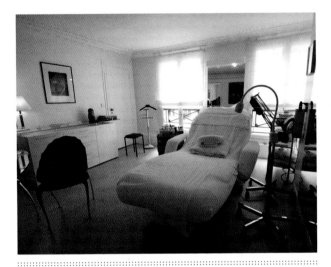

JOËLLE CIOCCO

8, place de la Madeleine, 8th arr.

✆ 01 42 60 58 80

Métro: Madeleine

Monday to Friday 9:30 am to 6:30 pm

www.joelle-ciocco.com (E)

Joëlle Ciocco: biologist, chemist, skin nutritionist, and *epidermologue*. Ciocco coined this last term to describe the science of analyzing and defining the skin's ecosystem to develop a plan of personalized skincare for it. Her confidential discrete space is tucked into a corner of Place de la Madeleine—the office is inconspicuous, but as you enter, an international, multilingual staff greets you enthusiastically and offers a hot cup of tea.

Ciocco practices *la haute* of skincare: made-to-measure protocols. Ideally, her clients visit seasonally so that skincare prescriptions can be monitored and adapted. Ciocco's products are naturally formulated from 100% vegetable and plant ingredients.

Guests receive an in-depth questionnaire that asks where they spend most of their time—inside, outside, at home or work—and how much they smoke, drink, and exercise. It also considers which type of transportation they use, contraception, medical history, sleep habits, and their skincare routine. This thorough look at a person's external and internal environment, coupled with a microscopic look at the epidermis, gives Joëlle Ciocco and her associates a glimpse into the skin's ecosystem. She encourages clients to pay attention to how their skin reacts to products. She says, "The skin should not have to adapt to cosmetic products—it should be the other way around." She works with a team of doctors and scientists to find the root cause of a skin condition and provide a holistic approach to treatment.

The center's menu includes massages, facials, nurturing manicures and pedicures, waxing, and eyebrow and eyelash tinting. A two-hour consultation and treatment with Joëlle Ciocco or one of her associates provides the basis for the prescription (320€–680€). She and her assistants offer a one-hour facial massage (130€) and an oxygen mask with Vitamin C (60€), as well as body therapies like the massage with omega oils (160€, 1 hour). Her products are available in a few select locations in Paris and abroad, including in New York. One of her best-selling products is the Lait Onctueux Capital, a face and neck cleanser made with orange flowers, calendula, arnica, and horsetail extract (47.50€, 3.4oz).

LA MAISON DE BEAUTÉ CARITA

11, rue du faubourg Saint-Honoré, 8th arr.

☎ 01 44 94 11 11

Métro: Concorde or Madeleine

Tuesday to Saturday 10 am to 6:30 pm

www.maisondebeautecarita.fr (E)

Maria and Rosy Carita were the first female hairdressers in the Paris market; the sisters created iconic looks for French stars such as Brigitte Bardot, Jean Seberg, and Catherine Deneuve before moving on to skincare. They looked to modernize the industry by creating lighter, more fluid products, and in 1951, they opened their salon at the fashionable 11, rue du faubourg Saint-Honoré. The *institut* is a modern space with impressive light and height.

The ground floor at Carita offers an initiation into the world of *haute beauté*, the philosophy behind the brand. It is the idea that "beauty artisans" should listen closely to their clients to precisely determine their needs in order to deliver a customized response. Express services like Belle du Jour, a makeup application (50€, 30 minutes), the Soin Modelage Pieds, a quick pedicure (50€, 30 minutes) and manicures are offered here. La Maison de Beauté offers top-notch body and facial services and is also a full-service hair salon.

The Séance Idéal Pro-Lift is a facial that uses the Pro-Lift tool— invented at Carita—to deeply clean the skin so it will be better prepared to receive facial products. The treatment works to smooth wrinkles and brighten skin (90€, 1 hour). The Caresse Volcanique & Peau Satin is one and a half hours of total escape: the body is exfoliated, then covered in a hydrating mixture made from essential oils, and finally wrapped. A therapist massages the face with cool pebbles and the body with warmed stones, and the result is velvety soft skin (160€). The Carita staff is charming and eager to reach out to customers, and reservations for treatments can be made online.

PYRÈNE
3 et 4, rue Greffulhe, 8th arr.
✆ 01 42 68 08 10
Métro: Madeleine
Monday, Wednesday, and Saturday 9:15 am to 8:30 pm,
Tuesday 8:30 am to 9 pm
www.institut-pyrene.com

ocated on a quiet street near the Madeleine, Pyrène offers a little bit of everything: it combines technology with natural products to occupy a niche space in the market. According to the spa director, the *institut* has two separate clienteles—one looking for well-being care that utilizes natural, organic products, and another who seeks permanent makeup and hair removal services. Pyrène uses the organic brand Phyt's (pronounced *feets*) exclusively in its facial and body treatments.

Pyrène has thirteen treatment rooms and is comprised of three separate spaces. One is dedicated to well-being treatments like massage and facials; one houses the space for permanent makeup and eyelash extension; one offers private coaching in Pilates and Power Plate.

The spa/salon menu includes *hammam* access, manicures, pedicures, waxing, and an array of slimming and cellulite treatments. The Lomi Lomi, inspired by a Hawaiian tradition, is a Parisian favorite. This therapy combines a series of movements that mirror the energy of the four elements: deep pressure for earth; light strokes for air; long, fluid movement for water; and large, expansive motions that unify the body for fire (85€, 1 hour). Vaulted ceilings and the use of natural fabrics and textures diminish the otherwise clinical feeling of the facility.

ROYAL THAÏ SPA
27, rue Pasquier, 8th arr.
✆ 01 40 06 08 59
Métro: Saint-Augustin or Madeleine
Monday to Saturday 11 am to 8 pm
http://www.royalthaispa.fr

The scent of jasmine pervades this chic center for traditional Thai massage, located just a few blocks from Place de la Madeleine. Buddha statues dot the space and bejeweled elephants rest on the table, while white river rocks and bamboo bring nature into the spa. A narrow stairway leads up to the treatment area, where silence is strictly observed. Guests are clothed for the traditional massage, which is performed in a communal area;

private treatment rooms are used for the oil and herbal compress massages, to preserve clients' privacy. Sheets and towels are provided to cover the body and ensure comfort.

Royal Thaï also specializes in reflexology for feet, head, and hands, and prepares therapeutic jasmine and honey baths in a pleasant downstairs room. A traditional Thai beauty ritual—a honey and sesame exfoliation treatment—is also available. There are five oversized rattan lounge chairs for foot massage off the reception area. Guests wait to be called for their service as they sip a cup of lemongrass tea. The staff is attentive, and the massage technique is effective at relieving pain and inspiring an overall improved sense of well-being. The traditional Thai massage is a standout (80€, 1 hour).

SOTHYS

128, rue du Faubourg-Saint-Honoré, 8th arr.
☎ 01 53 93 91 53
Métro: Saint-Phillipe-du-Roule or Miromesnil
Monday to Friday 9:30 am to 7:30 pm,
Saturday 9:30 am to 7 pm
www.sothys.com (E)

Sothys opened its first salon in Paris over sixty years ago. Its philosophy is based on the spa's signature method, Digi-Esthétique, which is a specific technique of manipulation designed to boost the skin's circulation and improve its appearance. Sothys' treatments avoid the use of devices, focusing instead on the human touch.

The impressive entrance to the *institut* is covered in black iron grilles, above which sits a golden image of Sothys, the Egyptian goddess after which the institute is named. According to myth, Sothys was the brightest star in the sky; to Egyptians, she symbolized eternal beauty. When Saturn turned his interest towards Sothys, Venus became enraged with jealousy. Venus took her revenge on Sothys and the star vanished from the sky into darkness. When she reappeared centuries later, Sothys dedicated herself to preserving the beauty and happiness of women on Earth.

Sothys offers limited-edition seasonal therapies in addition to massage and facials. The menu also includes makeup application and instruction, exfoliation treatments, slimming massages, hand and foot care, and hair removal. The Hanakasumi, one of Sothys' newest creations, begins with a cherry flower and rice powder exfoliation, followed by a foot massage designed to improve the body's energy flow. It ends with an Asian-scented shea butter massage (140€, 1 hour 10 minutes).

Sothys' men's salon shares the same address but has a separate entrance. The service and treatment style are more direct, and the interior has a business edge to it. The three-hour Escapade Sothys Homme is a comforting body massage that uses orange and marjoram essential oils and is followed by a detoxifying treatment (225€).

SPA GUERLAIN

68, avenue des Champs-Elysées, 8th arr.

✆ 01 45 62 11 21

Métro: George V or Franklin-D.-Roosevelt

Daily 9 am to 7 pm, Thursday until 9 pm, Friday until 8 pm

www.guerlain.fr (E)

Located on the bustling Champs-Elysées, Spa Guerlain is undeniably luxurious—and popular: guests must reserve spa treatment two to three weeks in advance. Entering the Guerlain complex from the street, the first two floors showcase Guerlain's selection of more than eighty perfumes. Upstairs, the tiny spa reception belies what is behind the flowing white curtains: a breathtaking interior, remodeled in 2005 by famed French interior designer Andrée Putman. Beyond the white sheers is a remarkably feminine space cloaked in white.

A huge relaxation room sits on the left, bathed in natural sunlight and decorated with white banquettes, white couches, and an extravagant chandelier—guests enjoy manicures and pedicures in this area. The hall that leads to the treatment rooms is equipped with an elongated white marble table stocked full of fluffy robes and towels; massive vases filled with fresh flowers sit on top. The spa has ten high-style treatment rooms.

Two services stand out: Le Soin Exceptionel Orchidée Impériale, a stimulating and detoxifying anti-aging facial that consists of two masks and a targeted treatment for the eye area (280€, 2 hours) and the Ordonnance Voyage: Décalage Horaire, a series of therapies designed to ease the strain of vigorous travel. A Guerlain Beauty Coach starts with an assessment of the client's nutritional, emotional, and physical needs. A forty-five-minute soak in a hydro-massage bathtub, Hydrothérapie des 5 sens, follows. During the bath, the guest is massaged with essential oils. The Drainage Lymphatique Esthétique, a sixty-minute massage that works to create movement of the lymph system and enhance circulation in the legs, is next. The final stage is an intensive hour-and-a-half-long pedicure with an exfoliation, massage, application of specialized masks and creams, and nail polish (395€, 3¼ hours). The salon offers slimming and firming body treatments, waxing, and hydrotherapy in addition to massages and facials.

Institut Guerlain has a mini-salon in Orly airport for abbreviated services, as well as a new location in Versailles.

Alternate Location:

SPA HÔTEL TRIANON PALACE

1, boulevard de la Reine, 78000 Versailles

✆ 01 30 84 50 00

U-SPA BARRIÈRE

In the Hôtel Fouquet's Barrière
46, avenue George V, 8th arr.
✆ 01 40 69 60 70
Métro: George V
Monday to Friday 10 am to 9 pm, Sunday 10 am to 8 pm
www.lucienbarriere.com/localized/fr/thalasso_spa/nos_
etablissements/uspa.htm (E)

Fouquet's U-Spa Barrière is as sumptuous and sophisticated as it gets in Paris. The hotel is steeped in Parisian history, but the spa is relatively new—it was completed in 2006. The staff is doting, and they all speak impeccable English. U-Spa is an ecologically minded urban well-being center. It takes care to conserve water, use environmentally sensitive products, and incorporate natural materials throughout the spa.

The décor is contemporary Asian, with teak walls, slate floors, and deep-brown mosaics. Facilities include an impressive swimming pool, saunas for men and women, a spectacular *hammam*, and a fitness room complete with Power Plate machines. There is a separate aqua-fitness course, with a bubble bath, waterfall, counter-current walkway and full-body underwater massage jets. Besides spa clients, hotel guests and club members have access to the pool and fitness areas. U-Spa offers fitness coaching, body wraps, manicures, pedicures, hair removal, and makeup application.

The spa menu is extensive, offering over forty treatments. Among U-Spa's signature therapies are the Terraké relaxing baths. These hydro-massage tubs use chromo- and aromatherapy to complement the soak. The Primordial Waters is a citrus-scented bath with

mandarin, lemon, and orange essential oils. For men, guaiacum and cardamom oils are used (65€, 30 minutes). A totally indulgent service exclusive to U-Spa is the U6, a massage with three therapists working simultaneously on the head, back, and feet (320€, 50 minutes). The Mer Originelle facial uses red algae and marine extracts from the Antarctic (107€, 1 hour).

The seven large treatment rooms are equipped with hi-tech heated beds. A mattress is placed directly on the floor for the traditional Thai and Indian massages. Sheer curtains that surround the treatment area within the room provide a nurturing veiled effect. Guests

are served with juices, teas, or water and fresh fruit in the relaxation area. The spa offers a lavish snack platter, the Palette of Delights, which can be taken by the pool (70€).

✘ U-Spa has a limited choice of items available to be eaten within the spa, but La Galerie Joy, a bar and casual restaurant upstairs, offers a handful of choices designated as "light and well-being." It has a outdoor garden and terrace, perfect for lounging in good weather. A Salade César (26€) or Saumon Fumé served with blinis, toast, and a mesclun salad (32€) are two light choices.

WASSANA

28, rue de Saint-Pétersbourg, 8th arr.
☎ 01 40 08 07 94
Métro: Place-de-Clichy
Monday to Saturday 11 am to 8 pm, Thursday until 9 pm
www.wassana-beauty.com

I f you have never experienced traditional Thai massage, a trip to Wassana can be life-altering. Madame Wassana began her career in Paris as a cook and restaurateur, and her Thai restaurants were so successful that she was able to realize her dream of opening a wellness center for traditional Thai massage. At the outset, it was not easy to convince the Parisian public of the virtues and legitimacy of the Thai tradition. As Madame Wassana puts it,

"the other" Thai massage had created unsavory connotations for Parisians—but she was soon to change their minds. Madame Wassana began massaging restaurant clientele and educating Parisians on the ancient style. Her client list quickly grew, and she opened Wassana Thaï Beauty Institute; it is the only *institut* officially recognized by the Thai embassy in Paris.

Traditional Thai massage or Nuad Bo-rarn has its roots in Thai and Ayurvedic medicine and dates back more than two thousand years. The massage is characterized by rhythmic, rocking motions that are combined with gentle stretching. The therapist moves in unison with the client's breathing pattern. Gradual yet firm pressure is applied along the body's acupressure points to promote better circulation (70€, 1 hour). The final result is a feeling of total well-being and relaxation, a sense of womb-like nurturing. All of the therapists at Wassana trained at Temple Wat Po, Bangkok's acclaimed center for traditional medicine and Thai massage.

There are two locations in the city, the original spa in the 8th and a second in the 16th arrondissement. The location in the 16th is warmly decorated and the space more intimate; it also has fewer facilities than the 8th, with no *hammam*. The 8th looks more familiar, like a grandmother's living room—but the staff is so hospitable that it has charm. The larger *institut* offers massage, including the *Wassanita* (a traditional Thai slimming massage), *hammam* sessions with exfoliation treatments, therapeutic baths, facials and body treatments, waxing, manicures, pedicures, and coloring services, as well as makeup application for daytime or night.

✗ Madame Wassana made her name in Paris first as a cook and restaurateur. If you reserve a treatment at the Wassana location in the 8th arrondissement, the spa will be happy to order in a meal from the nearby Wassana Thai restaurant. The chicken with green curry and coconut is mouth-watering (12€). Lighter selections include salads, like the shrimp salad seasoned with Thai herbs (11.50€).

9th Arrondissement

::

::

CENTRE UMA

14, rue Choron, 9th arr.

☎ 01 44 53 61 13

Métro: Notre-Dame-de-Lorette or Saint-Georges

Monday to Saturday, by appointment

www.uma-paris.com

Centre Uma is a busy neighborhood center that teaches prenatal and other yoga classes in a cozy and earthy setting. It also features Ayurvedic and Asian massage, Reiki, and consultations with Ayurvedic doctors. It is one of the few places in Paris for Gyrotonic training. Tea is available to guests as they wait in a sunlit reception area decorated with blue-flowered tiles from India. A small boutique sells natural well-being products.

As you descend the stairway to the treatment rooms, you'll notice that the area is softly lit by candles and that silence is fiercely respected. There are three rooms, plus an additional one upstairs with an Ayurvedic massage table used for the Shirodhara massage, in which a thin and regulated stream of warm herbal oil is poured steadily on the forehead to improve mental clarity and promote relaxation (130€, 45m). The Akshi Abhyanga involves a combination of the Abhyanga massage on the head and body, while the back is massaged with the traditional five-metal Kansu bowl. The treatment promotes deep relaxation (70€, 50m).

✕ The walk to Centre Uma, along the lively Rue des Martyrs, provides a great snapshot of traditional French food shops: a butcher and cheese shop, deli, bakery, and artisanal olive oil shop line this colorful street. A bit farther up the street from Centre Uma is Rose Bakery, a self-described "brunch, lunch, tea place" that offers a healthy and delicious selection of food; 80% of the menu is organic. Scones, house-made granola, pizzas, salads, and sweet or savory tarts have a devoted following among Parisians. Rose Bakery, 46, Rue des Martyrs, 9th arr. (01 42 82 12 80)

I-SPA BY ALGOTHERM

In the Grand Hôtel Intercontinental
2, rue Scribe, 9th arr.
✆ 01 40 07 32 32
Métro: Opéra
Daily 9 am to 8 pm
www.algotherm.fr

Immediately around the corner from the Opéra Garnier, spa enthusiasts can find a little piece of Bora Bora in Algotherm's I-Spa. The I-Spa occupies a relatively small space inside the Hôtel Intercontinental; a walk through the splendid hotel reception and atrium lounge is a stroll through elegance and luxury.

Algotherm was created in 1962 and is considered the pioneer of marine-based skincare products. One of the spa's signature packages is the Paris Time Zone, a series of therapies targeted to minimize the effects of jet lag. The guest begins in a hydro-massage bath that combines sea salts, seaweed, and essential oils to relieve fatigue and improve circulation after a long flight. It is followed by a special jet lag massage and finishes with a facial treatment personalized to the guest's skin type (208€, 2 hours 20 minutes). The Balade Polynésien is a series of treatments designed at the I-Spa in Bora Bora. After a therapeutic bath, sands imported from Bora Bora are used to exfoliate the body while reclining on a warm-water mattress, a treatment exclusive to I-Spa. Afterwards, the bed automatically lowers to create a sensation of being suspended. The series ends with a Polynesian Heï Poa massage (145€, 1½ hours).

The I-Spa is the only Parisian spa with a treatment that uses sea mud from Mont Saint-Michel, on the coast of Brittany in north-eastern France. Sea mud is prized for its high concentration of minerals, enzymes, and amino acids, which are absorbed through the skin (55€, 30 minutes). The spa also offers tanning, slimming and anti-cellulite treatments, nail care, waxing, makeup application, and access to its fitness center, sauna, and multi-sensory showers. Fruit juices and herbal teas, including a special detox tea created by the chef at the hotel, are served to refresh guests. The staff is friendly and, as at most palace hotels, speaks adequate to exceptional English.

MAXAM

34 bis, rue Vignon, 9th arr.

☎ 0 820 820 618

Métro: Madeleine

Monday to Saturday 10 am to 10 pm;

Sunday 11:30 am to 5:30 pm

www.maxam.cc

A bright and charming courtyard filled with bamboo and luscious greenery leads you to Maxam, a well-being center devoted to the best in healing arts from Asia: it offers massages from India, Thailand, Indonesia, Korea, China, and Japan. The six spacious treatment spaces are divided by country and decorated accordingly. The symbol that appears throughout the spa,

the Chinese ideogram that represents Maxam written in reverse, represents the perpetual return of spring. The spa was established after its owners traveled extensively in Asia and returned to France with a passion for Eastern massage techniques and culture; Maxam was voted the best Parisian spa in 2008 by spa professionals in Paris.

It is a clean and uncongested space, with Buddha statues and Burmese teak wood floors bordered by river rocks. The Chinese room is a dark and silent retreat decorated with red silk, black lacquer, and two red lanterns. Meditation music plays in the background; curtains, candles, and a subtle scent create a Zen ambience. A gorgeous, ornately carved wood façade encloses a relaxation room for the masseurs; it was designed in France and made in Bali. Fresh bamboo and rose petals line the stairwell down to the massage area.

Maxam offers massages for the body, face, feet, back, and stomach. The therapists use only natural products and 100% organic oils. It is the only spa in Paris to offer the three-hour Nuad Bo-rarn, traditional Thai massage (270€). Maxam is also unique in that one of its therapists is a Master of Kalaripayattu, the Indian martial art. He performs the Sukha, a Southern Indian massage technique designed to relieve muscular tension. The practitioner refines his technique with a series of questions and uses his hands and feet to apply pressure on vital points; the massage incorporates dance and martial art movement to improve blood circulation and flexibility and relieve pain (90€, 1 hour). Maxam also contains an on-site yoga studio where classes are offered. Reservations can be made from the U.S through the Spafinder website.

SPA CINQ MONDES

6, square de l'Opéra-Louis-Jouvet, 9th arr.

✆ 01 42 66 00 60

Métro: Opéra

Monday to Saturday 11 am to 8 pm,

Tuesday and Thursday until 10 pm

www.cinqmondes.com (E)

His passion for aromatherapy, massage, and natural cosmetics took founder of Spa Cinq Mondes, Jean-Louis Poiroux, on a ten-year quest in search of the world's best well-being treatments. The result of his research is Spa Cinq Mondes, or Five Worlds Spa, where treatments from five countries—China, Japan, Thailand, India, and Morocco—come together in one space.

Spa Cinq Mondes, a sophisticated spa concept with cosmopolitan sensibilities, has won countless awards and is considered among the top spas in Europe and the world, with additional locations in Monaco, Switzerland, and Morocco. The spa sells its own collection of products in its boutiques.

The Paris location is on a remarkably tranquil square near the Opéra Garnier. The color scheme at Cinq Mondes is dominated by white and warm pomegranate tones. The regular treatment rooms are comfortably sized; the double room is enormous. English is spoken, and the therapists are sensitive to issues of modesty. (Cinq Mondes is the only spa in Paris that asks, on a pre-service questionnaire, whether or not the client feels comfortable with the typical full-body massage in Paris—which includes the chest.)

The spa offers natural slimming and anti-cellulite treatments, massages and facials, manicures, pedicures, and an Asian waxing method that uses a honey paste. There is an authentic Japanese teak bath for therapeutic bathing, a *hammam*, and a space for body wraps and exfoliation treatments. The Rituel Royal du Siam is an indulgent series of treatments, beginning with a Japanese aromatic bath, followed by a papaya-based exfoliation, and ending with a relaxing Balinese massage (182€, 2 hours). Cinq Mondes' anti-cellulite therapy has a wide following. There are actually two creams available from the brand that target different kinds of cellulite. The spa uses La Crème de Café—a Brazilian recipe made with kola nut, green coffee, caffeine, and grapefruit acids—in a one-hour massage and body wrap that treats fatty cellulite (96€). La Crème Minceur Udvartana addresses cellulite caused from water retention (42€, 150ml).

The spa's product line is based on plant extracts from each of the five represented regions. The formulas use ancient well-being recipes adapted to the contemporary beauty space. Spa des Cinq Mondes' products are free from silicone, mineral oil, artificial coloring, and animal-based materials, and are tested under dermatological control. Their most popular product is Eau Egyptienne, a body spray based on an ancient recipe found at the Temple of Edfu in Egypt. The scent is made from 11 essential oils, including rose, mint, cumin, myrrh, geranium, and jasmine (48€, 100ml).

12th Arrondissement

OMNISENS

Bercy Village
23, rue des Pirogues-de-Bercy, 12th arr.
☎ 01 43 41 96 96
Métro: Cour Saint-Émilion
Monday to Saturday noon to 8 pm
www.omnisens.fr (E)

Omnisens is located just steps from Bercy Village, a district of nineteenth-century wine warehouses that have been restored and converted into shops and restaurants on the edge of the 12th arrondissement. It is a peaceful center of well-being that plays on the wine theme of neighboring Cour St. Émilion, the old wine distribution route.

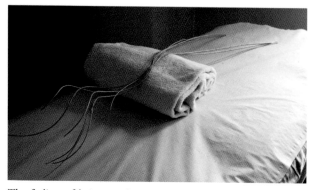

The feeling of being outdoors is a rare experience in a Parisian spa—but Omnisens isn't like other Parisian spas. On a clear day, sunlight pervades the space, which boasts high ceilings and a floor made from reclaimed chestnut wood, bordered with black river rocks. The therapy rooms look like small cabins built from white-washed planks. Omnisens uses its own product line, which is all-natural and free from parabens, mineral oil, and silicone.

Its Spa by Night package is popular for busy Parisians looking for a quick getaway: couples and friends arrive in the evening to a sampling of champagne and foie gras and enjoy spa services in a generously sized double room (238€, 2 hours). The Spa & Tea Time package for groups of two to four begins with time in the *hammam*, a relaxing thirty-minute massage, and finishes with a tea and *macaron* tasting (79€, 1½ hours). Guests leave with a complimentary bag of Omnisens products. The spa provides nail services in addition to massage, facials, and body treatments.

16th Arrondissement

MON SPA
In Mon Hôtel
1–3 rue d'Argentine, 16th arr.
✆ 01 45 02 76 76
Métro: Argentine
Daily 8 am to 9 pm, by appointment
www.monhotel.fr (E)

An intimate, full-service spa and salon, Mon Spa caters to one client at a time. It is located on a tranquil street in the 16th arrondissement in a recently renovated design hotel.

All services are provided in one space: a treatment area with black walls and a cloudy-sky ceiling floating above. A large screen projects restful and comforting images during the treatment. In addi-

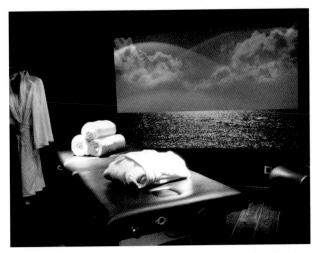

tion to body and facial treatments, Mon Spa offers hairdressing, waxing, and medical and esthetic nail care. In the hands of the skilled therapist, the Massage Aromatique aux Huiles Essentielles leaves the guest totally peaceful (90€, 1 hour). If you're interested in a novelty treatment, the Massage et Gommage au Chocolat is a nourishing massage and exfoliation that uses chocolate and cacao-based products (100€, 1 hour).

Mon Spa also has a small fitness space that offers private coaching and yoga instruction. The *hammam*, covered in blue mosaic tile and a ceiling that twinkles with fiber optic "stars," is lovely and private. Mon Hôtel continues the high-design theme in its hip bar-lounge, with black and rich purple color, oversized glass chandeliers, and huge canvases; it's a convenient stop for a cocktail or snack.

VILLA THALGO TROCADÉRO
8, avenue Raymond-Poincaré, 16th arr.
✆ 01 45 62 00 20
Métro: Trocadéro
Daily; call for specific hours
www.villathalgo.fr/en (E)

Completed in the summer of 2009, Villa Thalgo Trocadéro is a gorgeous example of the modern Parisian spa. This fitness club and spa is filled with every technology imaginable, including extensive chromotherapy lighting. Villa Thalgo has brought a marine ambience to this refined 9,000-square-foot space near Trocadéro. A large swimming pool projects mesmerizing images for swimmers. Mosaic tile in aquatic colors,

walls textured with sand, a stairway accented with copper and driftwood, a wave-sculpted wall that moves through the spa: nothing was overlooked to bring the sea inside.

The spa is divided into three areas: Toning, which includes the fitness center and aqua-gym; Relaxing, which includes the swimming pool, lounge, and patio; and Treatment, which includes therapy rooms, the *hammam*, and a relaxation room. The *hammam* is spectacular, with slate-colored mosaic tiles, a ceiling that sparkles with fiber optic lights, and expansive space that includes a water basin in the center diffusing sea salts and the scent of salt water. Exfoliation treatments use a remineralizing algae-based product instead of the traditional black soap.

The spa offers two rooms with therapeutic baths that work with video screens and chromotherapy; the swimming pool and seven other treatment rooms, which include one luxurious VIP suite, also use the light-based therapy. In addition to spa services, also available are manicures, pedicures, makeup, waxing, and slimming treatments; there is a separate spa menu for men. The spa is accessible to those with limited mobility.

In June 2009, Thalgo released a collection of organic skincare products that Villa Thalgo has integrated into their services. Le Soin Bio Terre et Mer facial combines essential oils with preserved algae to nourish the skin (95€, 1¼ hours). The Aquazen aux Ballons d'Eau is a massage exclusive to Villa Thalgo that uses balloons filled with warm water to relax muscles and relieve tension (10€, 50 minutes).

✗ The state-of-the-art Villa Thalgo spa and fitness club has a simple on-site café, The Lounge Bar, with a solid choice of seasonal salads, quiches, desserts, teas, smoothies, and infusions. The mango and passion fruit or the raspberry and blackberry smoothie are refreshing (5€). La Salade Vitalité is made with lettuce, avocado, grapefruit, cherries, smoked salmon and tossed in a citrus vinaigrette (15€). In case you are unable to completely sever the cord with the outside world, don't fear—the café has Wi-Fi access.

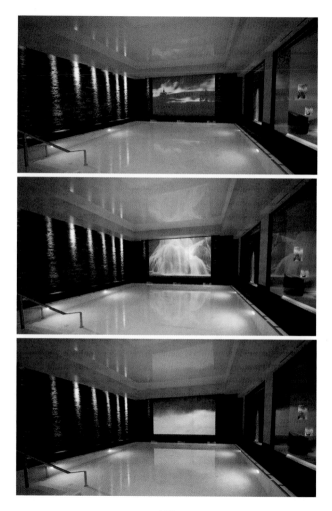

Suburban Paris

::

HAMMAM LES CENT CIELS

45 bis, avenue Édouard-Vaillant, 92100 Boulogne-Billancourt

✆ 01 46 20 07 01

Métro: Porte-de-Saint-Cloud or Marcel-Sembat

Monday 10 am to 5 pm, Wednesday 11 am to 11 pm,

Thursday and Friday 10 am to 5 pm, Saturday 10 am to 9 pm,

Sunday 10 am to 8 pm

www.hammam-lescentciels.com

H ammam Les Cent Ciels brings a piece of North Africa into its vast spa, which houses the largest *hammam* in Europe. The authentic décor features objects collected during the travels of Cent Ciels' creators, Véronique and Jean-Michel Bonnefont; many of the interior materials were imported

from Morocco. The comfy spa café has a retractable ceiling that can be opened on days when the weather is nice. Les Cent Ciels is in the process of opening a new location in central Paris, near the Bastille area.

Bonnefont infused an East-meets-West aesthetic into the space to make the *hammam* ritual more accessible to Parisians and other Westerners. The *hammam*'s mosaic-covered interior is superb, and it includes a novel twist: the cool *hammam*. In it, a cooling mist replaces the traditional hot steam. The space features exfoliation rooms, seven massage areas (the loveliest of them flank the swimming pool), and a sauna. The Rituel Éclat Plus is a package with *hammam*, sauna, and pool time, black soap and eucalyptus exfoliation for the body, a Rassoul and essential oil body treatment, and a reenergizing fifteen-plant facial mask (85€). If it is your first time in a *hammam*, the Rituel Initiation is a good start; it grants access to the *hammam*, sauna, and swimming pool (40€).

The spa has two large relaxation rooms dimly lit by candles; one room is darker than the other, designed for those in search of a deeper rest. The ceiling is covered in a sheath of ornately carved metal; mustard-yellow fabrics accent the reception and hallways, and Moroccan chandeliers and colored lamps hang overhead. Cent Ciels is a twenty-minute ride from the center of Paris, but the spacious *hammam* is a good place for steam-bath debutantes, as it provides enough space for privacy and anonymity.

✗ Les Cent Ciels designed its spa from the ground up and included a café-lounge with a retractable roof and upstairs terrace. The café serves light Middle Eastern–inspired fare, including a tagine of the day, and juices and a variety of teas, coffees, and wine.

SPA AQUATONIC PARIS VAL D'EUROPE

15, avenue des Fresnes, 77144 Montevrain

✆ 01 60 31 01 01

RER Line A, Marne La Vallée/Chessy, Gare: Val d'Europe

Monday to Saturday 10 am to 8 pm, Sunday 10 am to 6 pm

www.spa-aquatonic-paris-valdeurope.com (E)

When the founders of Les Thermes de Saint-Malo decided to select a spot for a marine and aqua-centered well-being space in the Paris area, they chose Montevrain, thirty minutes from the city center. It is located just minutes from EuroDisney and the corporate parks that occupy this suburb, and sits next to the four-star Home Business Hotel, connected directly to the spa through an underground passage. Spa Aquatonic opened in 2009 and caters to an international clientele. Built from the ground up, it integrates the latest in spa technology.

The center of attraction at Aquatonic is the Parcours, an enormous aquatic fitness course with fourteen different segments. There are jets that massage each part of the body—one of the most soothing runs from the ankles up to the shoulders and then back down again. The Parcours includes a bubble bath, swan fountains that massage the shoulders, a counter-current path, and an outdoor Jacuzzi that is connected to the interior pool (30€, 25€ with reserved spa service).

The spa is decorated in neutral, earthy tones, and the large windows welcome the natural light. The treatment rooms are well sized and equipped with comfortable warmed massage tables. The coastal theme is understated, and the scent of Les Thermes' marine-based products is pleasantly subtle. Aromatherapy is incorporated into the *hammam* and relaxation room, where guests rest on warming waterbed loungers. Chromotherapy is used in the "multi-sensorial" showers, Jacuzzi, and relaxation room; the Jacuzzi has cool and heated sections. Sauna and fitness areas are also available. Guests can prearrange to have lunch in the lounge area, where water, juices, coffee, tea, and fresh fruit are served for refreshment.

The treatment menu is extensive, with dozens of facials and massages, body wraps, services with Vichy showers, and therapeutic baths; Aquatonic offers a huge selection of packages for both individuals and couples. The Soin Éclat Marin (Marine Radiance Facial) treats dull skin with spirulina, horsetail, and an oxygenating massage (105€, 1 hour 10 minutes). Jeunesse et Silhouette combines slimming and anti-aging therapies, and access to the well-being area: *hammam*, sauna, Jacuzzi, chromotherapy showers, and relaxation room. The day package includes a Marine Anti-Aging and Marine Contouring treatment, in which a massage and body wrap containing active marine extracts are followed by a facial that uses marine collagen and hydrolyzed elastin to firm skin (205€, 3 hours). For those in the Paris area who do not have time for a four-hour trip to Les Thermes de Saint-Malo, Spa Aquatonic is the next best thing.

SPA VINOTHÉRAPIE CAUDALIE

Les Étangs de Corot

53–55, avenue de Versailles, 92410 Ville d'Avray

✆ 01 41 15 37 00

Monday to Sunday 10 am to 7 pm

See note below re: transportation

www.caudalie-usa.com/site/caudalie_spa_paris.html (E)

The bucolic setting of Les Étangs de Corot, a large pond surrounded by trees and foliage, is just a short distance from Versailles and twenty minutes from Paris. The hotel and spa sit on one side of the pond, with calming views and first-rate facilities. The area was a serene retreat for nineteenth-century artists and writers who wanted a break from city life—the painter

Corot lived in a neighboring house and painted scenes of this idyllic spot. Les Étangs feels a world away from Paris.

The spa was inspired by the Caudalie skincare brand, which capitalizes on the anti-oxidant properties of polyphenols found in grape skins and seeds. Most of the raw materials for the products come from the owner's family's winemaking estate, Smith Haut Lafitte, near Bordeaux. The name Caudalie refers to the time a wine's aftertaste lingers in one's mouth—instead of a second, the unit of time is called a *caudalie*.

The spa was designed by the same architect responsible for Caudalie's other spas in Bordeaux, New York, and Spain. It is a space filled with natural light that overlooks the small lake; each of the seven treatment rooms has a view of the water. The colors are muted

grays and cabernet, with dark Brazilian wood and pink mosaic accents. The spacious VIP suite is home to a hydro-massage barrel bath that looks like a huge wine vat. Guest can soak in a fifteen-minute Bain Barrique à la Vigne Rouge—a bath enriched with red vine extracts (60€).

The spa has a *hammam*, two relaxation lounges, and a large whirlpool. Guests are served grapes and herbal tea as refreshment. Spa services include body wraps, baths, manicures, pedicures, facials, and massage. The Crushed Cabernet Scrub uses grape seeds combined with honey, brown sugar, and essential oils to exfoliate the skin (80€, 35 minutes). The Vinoperfect Treatment is an anti-aging facial that uses Caudalie's Vinexpert line, which contains Resveratrol, the ingredient in wine that fights free radicals (100€, 50 minutes).

Caudalie products are available in French *pharmacies* and throughout the world. The spa is best reached by taxi or private transportation, but is also accessible from Paris via the commuter train.

Note: Although Spa Vinothérapie Caudalie is accessible by commuter train from the Gare St-Lazare, it is not recommended. Although taking a taxi from Paris is expensive, it is a much more comfortable and convenient option.

✘ The Café des Artistes at the spa-hotel serves tapas and bistro fare, as well as wine and an afternoon tea service. The service could be better, but with prime views of the pond, the setting is unbeatable.

LA SULTANE DE SABA

22, rue Lejemptel, 94300 Vincennes

✆ 01 48 08 19 09

Métro: Château de Vincennes

Monday to Friday 10:30 am to 7:30 pm, Thursday 11 am to 9 pm

www.lasultanedesaba.com (E)

A visit to La Sultane de Saba is a total immersion into the beauty rites and recipes of Morocco, Egypt, India, and Indonesia. The spa's creator, Vanessa Sitbon, developed this 100% natural, paraben-free product line and based its formulas on authentic beauty recipes of Eastern queens and royalty. The spas have expanded rapidly since 1995, and La Sultane now has three locations in Paris. The newest is located in Vincennes, a suburb

adjacent to the city. The locations in the 2nd arrondissement and Vincennes are preferred for their ambience and authentic décor.

The Vincennes spa is filled with exotic treasures gathered on trips to the Middle East: Syrian pearl chandeliers, Moroccan lamps, and banquettes covered in sumptuous fabrics. Before heading to the treatment rooms, the therapist explains the virtues of different oils, and one is chosen depending on the guest's tastes and immediate needs. A stairway lit with candles leads downstairs to the spa, where the décor is black with gold accents. The treatment rooms are small. The relaxation room is a beautiful space, with beaded chandeliers and black couches piled with gold-embroidered cushions. La Sultane's captivating *hammam* is covered in pearly black mosaic and accommodates up to six people. Guests are served a refreshing mint tea and pastry after their treatment and encouraged to take all the time necessary to unwind.

Sultane's signature services include a full-body Henna spray tanning treatment (35€) and Soin à la Rose et au Miel et Galets, a rose and honey hydrating facial (55€, 1 hour). One of the better values on the Parisian spa scene is La Détente à l'Orientale. This package includes access to the *hammam*, face and body black soap *gommage* (scrub), a soothing application of shea butter and Rassoul, a light twenty-minute massage with essential oils, and finally a facial mask (105€, 1½ hours). If you are curious about experiencing the *hammam* and the skincare rituals associated with it, La Sultane de Saba gives guests a thorough introduction within a discreet setting.

The shelves of the boutique in the reception area are lined with Sultane's beauty products. The black soap scrubs, made from Mo-

roccan olives, are its bestsellers; they leave the skin remarkably soft and moisturized (20€–26€, 300g). An easy weekly at-home scrub yields similar results to the *gommage* performed after the *hammam*. La Sultane's products are sold throughout Europe, the Middle East, and Asia, with limited distribution in the United States.

Alternate locations:

8, rue Bachaumont, 2nd arr.
✆ 01 40 41 90 95

78, rue Boissière, 16th arr.
✆ 01 45 00 00 40

Thermalisme, Hammam & Thalassotherapy

The therapeutic use of water has played an important role in the life of Paris from antiquity through today. Its contemporary use incorporates different ethnic traditions as well as those developed in France.

Thermalisme is the therapeutic use of mineral water or water from hot springs. Roman public baths were constructed around hot springs, or water was brought in via aqueducts. The origins of water-based therapies in Paris date back to Les Thermes de Cluny, public baths created by the Romans between the 2nd and early part of the 3rd century, still partially standing along Boulevard Saint-Germain. The water that served Cluny was brought in along the Arcueil aqueduct from east of the city. The baths were made up of three principal areas: the *caldarium* (hot bath), the *tepidarium* (warm bath), and the *frigidarium* (cold bath). Roman baths were more elaborate than those of their Greek predecessors, and included gymnasiums, swimming pools, and areas for massage and changing. The baths were open to everyone and became an important part of social life and basic hygiene. There were multiple public bath complexes in Paris. The remains of another bath complex, known as Les Thermes de l'Est, also called Les Thermes du Collège de France, lie along the rue des Écoles in Paris's Latin Quarter, and yet another, Les Thermes de la rue Gay-Lussac, in the same area.

Today, the Musée du Moyen Age is partly located in the *frigidarium* of the Cluny site. Invading Barbarians near the end of the 3rd century destroyed the baths at Cluny; today, the ruins can be seen at the corner of Boulevard Saint-Michel and Boulevard Saint-Germain from the street through the iron fence. (Musée national du Moyen Âge - Thermes et Hôtel de Cluny, 6, place Paul Painlevé, 75005 Paris, Tel. 01 53 73 78 00, Métro: Cluny-La Sorbonne, Saint-Michel, or Odéon, Daily except Tuesday 9:15 am to 5:45 pm. Closed January 1, May 1, and December 25, www. musee-moyenage.fr/ang/index.html)

In France today, more than 550,000 people each year undergo a *cure* at *les thermes*. In addition to water, *thermalisme* includes the use of gas and mud from the same sources. There are approximately 120 centers for *thermalisme* in France.

Thermalisme is used to treat respiratory, rheumatic, circulatory, metabolic, and skin disorders. Various methods are utilized during a *cure*, including thermal baths and showers combined with massage and physical therapy, gas inhalation, and mineral water compresses.

The French medical system covers between 70% and 100% of a patient's stay at a thermal center. *Une cure thermale*, a treatment prescribed by a medical doctor, lasts twenty-one days. Once on site, a patient meets several times with a doctor who specializes in *thermalisme*. Because the government regulates the centers and the treatment environments can be warm and humid, a "zero bacteria" policy is enforced.

Hammam is a hot steam bath popular in parts of North Africa and the Middle East. In Paris, the ritual has caught on as a relaxing and detoxifying experience and guests will find a *hammam* in most spas and in some instituts. Today, there are *hammams* in every district in Paris.

Hammams have days of the week reserved uniquely for men and for women, and other days that are mixed. Bathing suits—or, at the very least, a bikini bottom—are almost always required. Be sure to check the spa's schedule and *hammam* protocol before showing up.

Hammams are divided into two or three areas. A person begins in the warm room and, after acclimating to the temperature, enters the hot room for more intense heat. The *hammam* uses humid heat—as opposed to the dry heat characteristic of a sauna—and varies between 95 and 110 degrees Farenheit. Guests sit or recline on tiled benches; some *hammams* have cool showers in the warm room. After about thirty to forty-five minutes, the pores have opened and the skin is ready for a *gommage*, or scrub. Women wearing exfoliation gloves use a traditional black soap to vigorously exfoliate the body. The body is then rinsed with cool water to close the pores. Many spas offer a gentle massage with essential oils in their basic *hammam* packages. The final stop is the relaxation area for a cup of tea and a pastry. The skin feels baby-soft after the ritual. *Hammams* have varied restrictions, but in general they are not advised for claustrophobics, people with serious disease, or those with cardio-vascular issues.

Balnéothérapie is a broad term that refers to the treatment of disease or health problems through bathing. In France, the therapy involves the use of water sources that are naturally rich in minerals, such as sulfur, magnesium, calcium, and potassium. These minerals nourish the skin and, although the claim is unsubstantiated by research, it is believed that they pass into the bloodstream with positive metabolic implications. *Balnéothérapie* can include a variety of methods, including hot, vapor, or mud baths. Thalassotherapy is a form of this therapy, but uses seawater instead of mineral water.

The term thalassotherapy comes from the Greek word *thalasso*, or "sea." It was developed in the coastal towns of Brittany in the 19th century and exploited the benefits of mineral-rich seawater for therapeutic purposes. Today, thalasso facilities exist on all of France's coasts. Contemporary centers in Brittany have signed a charter, overseen by the government, to ensure quality control. Government-approved centers require that the seawater be drawn from a specified distance and depth to guarantee its purity.

The therapy centers on the belief that when the body is submerged in seawater, the skin's pores absorb the minerals and salt present in the water, which then pass into the bloodstream to nourish the body from the inside out. Seawater is pumped directly from the sea and stored in containers for a maximum of twenty-four hours to preserve its active ingredients. It is believed that the seawater must be heated close to the body's temperature for the therapy to be effective. Thalasso includes algae therapy, the application of seaweed or seaweed baths, seawater showers and baths, and the inhalation of seawater vapors.

In France, thalassotherapy is used to treat arthritis, skin conditions like psoriasis and eczema, back pain, and metabolic disorders. A typical course of therapy, or *cure*, lasts six days. With modern budget cuts in the French medical system, however, the seawater treatments are no longer subsidized to the same extent as *thermalisme* (hot spring therapy). Thalassotherapy is currently regarded more as a recreational activity than as a medical therapy.

The following spas specialize in hydrotherapy, which includes hot spring therapies and thalassotherapy. Though they require a day or overnight trip from Paris, they are sources for an authentic thermal or seawater treatment.

SPARK AND LES THERMES
D'ENGHIEN-LES-BAINS

87, rue du Général-De-Gaulle, 95880 Enghien-les-Bains

☎ 01 39 34 10 50

Les Thermes Telephone: 01 39 34 10 57

Daily 10 am to 8 pm (spa treatments);
7:30 am to 10 pm (fitness facilities)

www.lucienbarriere.com (E)

::

The picturesque suburb of Enghien-les-Bains is located about 10 minutes from the French capital. This wealthy town has been known since the 18th century for its scenic lake and hot springs. In 1766, a priest discovered a warm sulfur spring near the water; in the 19th century, Enghien was developed as a spa resort and became a convenient retreat for Paris' middle class. As tourism expanded, the town built casinos and developed a lucrative gaming industry. Today, Enghien-les-Bains is the only therapeutic thermal station in the Paris region; it also has the casino closest to the city.

Barrière, the group that created the stunning U-Spa at Fouquet's in Paris (see page 113), developed the Spark well-being center in Enghien-les-Bains. The complex is an expansive 38,000-square-foot spa, fitness center, aquatic gym, and therapeutic center. The ground floor is a medical center; the spa occupies the two levels above.

Barrière manages Les Thermes, the medical center that uses the local sulfur spring to treat respiratory and voice disorders in adults and children. Many post-operative patients are sent to the Les Thermes as part of their recovery. The principal activity of Les Thermes is treating ear, nose, and throat problems, but there is also a space with bathing therapies devoted to those who suffer from arthritis. The center also offers therapies to help cope with stress, smoking cessation, and voice reeducation. An 18-day program for ear, nose, and throat therapy that includes six daily treatments starts at 409€, not including lodging. The facility is appropriately clinical, but it is also bright, clean, and spacious.

The name Spark is taken from the English word "sparkling," and was chosen to describe the modern and energetic ambience of the center. In planning this impressive temple to well-being, Barrière was inspired by the "relaxing benefits of Roman baths." Facilities include an aquatic fitness course, generously sized swimming pool, sauna, and *hammam*. There are 24 treatment rooms, some of which include Vichy showers and hydro-massage bathtubs. The VIP room for couples has a double bath and double shower. The spa features facials, massages, manicures, pedicures, slimming treatments, body wraps, and exfoliation. Le Sparkling is Spark's signature massage, adapted to the mood and needs of the client (95€, 1 hour). There is a choice of three therapeutic baths, Eaux Bienfaisantes, which include a 30-minute soak accompanied by individualized chromotherapy effects (60€, 30 minutes). A full-service salon is also located within the complex. A casual on-site café-restaurant serves healthy food. The staff is accommodating and there is a pleasant view of the lake.

THALASSO & SPA BY ALGOTHERM
AT DEAUVILLE
3, rue Sem, 14800, Deauville
☎ 33 02 31 87 72 00
Monday to Friday 9:15 am to 7 pm, Saturday 8:45 am to 7 pm,
Sunday 8:45 am to 2 pm.
www.thalasso-deauville.com/fr/index.html

D eauville is a seaside town, two hours northeast of Paris, which lies along the coast of Normandy. It has been a peaceful retreat for the rich and famous since the 19th century. With luxury hotels and casinos, it has become an accessible beach getaway for weekend tourists from Paris. The city is also known for its annual American Film Festival, held late each summer, which attracts a crowd of international film stars.

The Thalasso & Spa by Algotherm is a well-appointed spa and medical retreat with fantastic views of the sea. It is one of the most highly regarded centers for thalasso and is only a day trip away from Paris.

The Algotherm center is a huge complex, with 35 treatment rooms organized around four distinct spaces. It includes a full-service salon, a spa with an elaborate treatment menu, a fitness center, and a thalassotherapy facility. The Douche à Jets Harmonie du Corps is a therapy in which a hydro-therapist directs a stream of seawater at the client, who stands at a distance. The temperature of the water varies with the therapeutic requirements of the guest. The therapist begins spraying at the feet and works his or her way up to the neck to stimulate the circulatory and lymphatic systems (33€, 10 minutes). The Découverte is a day-trip-worthy package that combines a fresh algae bath, a Douche à Jets, and the choice of an algae-based body wrap or a sea mud application (101€, 1 hour). The packages all include access to the fitness areas. The center also offers medical *cures* that last between two and six days and include lunch and accommodations (270€ to 917€).

THERMES MARINS DE SAINT-MALO—
THALASSOTHERAPY CENTER AND SPA RESORT

100 Blvd Hébert, 35400 Saint Malo

✆ 33 02 99 40 75 75

Open Monday to Saturday 10 a.m. to 1 p.m. and 4 p.m. to
8:15 p.m., Sunday 10 a.m. to 1 p.m. and 3 p.m. to 7 p.m.

www.thalassotherapy.com (E)

The breathtaking fortified coastal city of Saint-Malo is a 3½-hour trip from Paris. The ramparts and old city have been stunningly preserved and give impressive views of the English Channel. One of the oldest thalasso centers, Les Thermes Marins de Saint-Malo opened in 1963. It sits regally along the Brittany coast and enjoys seaside views. Les Thermes de Saint-Malo is a thriving name in the world of marine-based skincare and thalassotherapy.

The center is elegantly mature, with 14 treatment rooms and facilities for all types of seawater therapies. The heated seawater therapeutic and aqua-fitness course includes 10 separate segments: hydro-jets for massaging each part of the body, "swan" fountains that extend out of the pool to massage shoulders, massage seats, bubble baths, and a counter-current walkway (25€, includes access to the *hammam*). The complex has a fitness gym, pool for aqua training, sauna, and *hammam*.

The spa menu is long: slimming, draining, exfoliation treatments, and body wraps are all available. The Escapade Thalasso is a weekend package that includes a choice of four treatments per day and full access to the facilities including the Aquatonic aqua-fitness and therapy pool (215€-315€ per person, depending on accommodation).

CHROMOTHERAPY

Chromotherapy is an alternative therapy that uses color and light to balance a person's energy. In most of the new French spas, chromotherapy lights are used in private treatment rooms and communal spaces to enhance the well-being experience.

The colors and their associations are rooted in Ayurvedic medicine:

Red: stimulates the mind and body, increases circulation.

Orange: increases energy levels and treats depression.

Yellow: stimulates creativity and the digestive system.

Green: calms and stabilizes, treats stress and insomnia.

Blue: relaxes and soothes.

Indigo: promotes inspiration, combats anxiety.

Violet: treats depression and migraines.

The following spas have incorporated chromotherapy extensively into their facilities and treatments:

Manicure & Pedicure

A few words about nail care: the French regard weekly salon visits for manicures and pedicures as peculiarly American, and although they regard the American enthusiasm for perfectly manicured and polished nails a bit obsessive, cosmetic nail care is catching on in Paris. Curiously, only a handful of salons offer nail care exclusively, but almost every spa offers a full menu of nail treatments. The busiest season for pedicures arrives with sandal weather in May or June, and during winter school vacations when many families head off to warmer climates. Book early during these periods.

Nail-care terms in France differ from those in America. Most salons and spas offer *la beauté des mains* or *le soin des mains*, which is what Americans consider a no-frills manicure: hands and nails are cleaned, and nails are clipped, shaped, and buffed. The service usually involves a moisturizer, but typically does not include nail polish. You will usually notice a separate charge for *pose vernis*, or nail polish application (4€–15€). In large spas and those that cater to an international clientele, the word *manucure* is used. As the price increases, so does the extent of services. More expensive treatments typically will include an exfoliation and hand massage. If you are expecting a massage or exfoliation, be sure to ask whether the *beauté des mains* includes a *massage* or *gommage*.

La beauté des pieds or *soin des pieds* is a cosmetic pedicure. The word *pédicure* has a medical connotation in France, and is sometimes clarified as a *pédicure médicale*. Professionals who perform this treatment are podiatrists or certified specialists who receive special training to work with a blade to trim dead skin or more serious skin growths. The details of the service will be clarified in its description.

AU STUDIO

17, rue Roquepine, 8th arr.
☏ 01 42 66 21 72
Métro: Saint-Augustin or Miromesnil
Monday to Friday 9 am to 8 pm,
Saturday by appointment 10 am to 5 pm
www.au-studio.com

A tiny shoebox of a reception area belies the depth of Au Studio's services and products. It is a colorful little shop with raspberry walls and black chandeliers, and behind the reception area is a series of treatment areas. Owner Eugénie Cani and her staff are welcoming and helpful. Hands and feet are the focus here, but Au Studio also offers waxing, makeup services, and facials. Au Studio is the only salon in Paris to use the Nail Station brand of products—the salon's clientele swears by it. Au Studio carries more than 350 colors. During pedicure season, which coincides with school vacations and sandal weather, appointments should be booked two to three weeks in advance. The staff is not quite fluent in English, but pointing and appropriate gestures will go a long way.

Une manucure simple includes a nail soak, cleaning, filing, a light hand and arm massage, and nail polish (30€, 45 minutes). *Une manucure complet* includes all of the basics of the *simple* as well as an exfoliation and massage with deliciously scented shea butter (53€, 1 hour). For the feet, Au Studio has services that range from the most basic to the lavish. La Beauté des Pieds Complète combines a footbath, nail grooming, foot and lower leg massage, and nail polish (53€, 1 to 1¼ hours).

MANUCURIST

4, rue de Castellane, 8th arr.

☎ 01 42 65 19 30

Métro: Tuileries or Pyramides

Monday to Saturday 10 am to 7 pm

www.manucurist.com

With three locations in Paris, Manucurist is known as one of the best spots for American-style nail service. In a city where heading to a salon for a manicure or pedicure is often a seasonal event, Manucurist stays busy year-long. It is a modern space, with bright lacquer colors, black tables, and a hip and youthful vibe. The Castellane location near Madeleine has four manicure and two pedicure stations. The shop features more than two hundred colors of Essie and Orly brand polish—everything from classic to neon hues. Manucurist is *the* spot for "Le French," an airbrushed French pedicure. The service is friendly and treatments are superb.

Le Soin Beauté Complet de Vos Mains is a complete manicure with nail and cuticle care, a hand massage with a soothing, warm cream, and nail polish (39€, 45 minutes). The French airbrush is an additional 4€. Pedicure stations are platform lounge chairs with a jetted footbath. Le Soin Expert Manucurist Pour des Pieds Parfaits is a pedicure with nail care, a foot and leg massage, and polish (53€, 1 hour). Manucurist also provides acrylic and gel nail application and touch-up.

Alternate Locations:

42, place du Marche St. Honoré, 1st arr.
✆ 01 42 61 03 81

13, rue de la Chaussée d'Antin, 9th arr.
✆ 01 47 03 37 33

PÉDICURE CHINOIS PANG WEI

13, rue de Laborde, 8th arr.

✆ 01 45 22 22 52

Métro: Saint-Augustin or Saint-Lazare

Monday to Saturday 9 am to 6:30 pm

::

Pang Wei is a house of healing for weary feet abused by poor-fitting shoes and big-city walking. This podiatrist works his magic in a petite boutique, and he comes by his talent honestly: he is the third generation in his family to carry on the art of the Chinese pedicure in Paris. Pang's grandfather worked in the famous Carita sisters' salon in the 1960s.

Pang Wei and his wife do all of their work by hand—without fancy electrics, jetted footbaths, or, traditionally, nail polish. His expert, efficient hands treat all of the unmentionables: ingrown toenails, calluses, and the delicate removal of corns. The service ends with a soothing massage and a coat of polish if desired (33€, 30 minutes).

SEPHORA CHAMPS-ELYSÉES NAIL BAR

70–72, avenue Champs-Elysées, 8th arr.

☎ 01 53 93 22 50

Métro: George V or Franklin-D.-Roosevelt

Sunday to Thursday 10 am to midnight,

Friday and Saturday 10 am to 1 am

www.sephora.fr

A visit to the Sephora shop on the Champs-Elysées is an experience in sensory overload. It is colossal, brightly lit, packed with shoppers, and loud with blaring music. Still, it is a great address to have in hand for a quick manicure or for a forgotten or lost beauty product. The staff's English capability varies widely, but everyone is eager to help. The nail bar is located towards the back of the store; it offers a full menu of hand care, including a simple polish (7€), manicure with polish (23€), or the application of a set of gel nails (60€). Sephora nail techs get lots of practice and operate with well-trained hands. Clients are advised to make reservations two to three days in advance.

The most attractive aspect of Sephora is that it is a one-stop beauty shop offering a variety of services available without reservations. At a small makeup kiosk techs can do a quick daytime makeup (10€, 10 minutes), evening makeup (15€, 15 minutes) or "smoky eyes" effect (15€). Another station can curl or straighten hair (15€), or style it for a wedding (45€). The Benefit Brow bar (*bar à sourcils*) offers an express eyebrow wax (21€, 20 minutes) and the staff at the Make Up For Ever bar will apply a set of classic or trendy eyelashes in a blink (18€).

SHU UEMURA NAIL BAR (BAR À ONGLES)

In Le Bon Marché department store
24, rue de Sèvres, 7th arr.
☏ 01 42 22 33 49
Métro: Sèvres-Babylone
Monday, Tuesday, Wednesday, and Saturday 10 am to 8pm;
Thursday and Friday 9pm

The Shu Uemura name is legendary in cosmetics; the famous makeup artist is known for bringing a sense of art to the makeup world. His eponymous nail bar, located on the ground floor of Le Bon Marché department store, is a good spot for a spontaneous nail service. This was the first nail bar to open in Paris and an innovative concept at the time. The space is designed to partition guests discreetly to provide a sense of privacy. A gracious host welcomes you into a bright lounge space with glossy red accents, then invites you to rest in one of the comfortable leather armchairs. Hot green tea is served, the nail service is selected, and a moment of Zen is underway.

The Japanese Manucure is a serious moment of escape in which nails are soaked, cleaned, trimmed, shaped, and buffed, and hands and forearms are massaged with nourishing oil made from cherry blossoms (45€, 45 minutes). Nail polish is an additional charge of 15€, and the Shu Uemura nail bar stocks more than 150 colors. The Grand Soin Réparateur elaborates on the basic manicure and includes a soak in a regenerating bath (60€, 1¼ hours). The twenty-minute express manicure, in which nails are meticulously cleaned and polished, is available without a reservation (32€).

In addition to the location at Le Bon Marché, Shu Uemura has a large makeup boutique on Boulevard Saint-Germain. The shop offers makeup classes and makeup application services for every occasion. The individualized course meets twice: the first time for instruction (1½ hours), the second for hands-on practice (1 hour) under the watchful eye of a trained expert (200€). The boutique also offers a workshop designed to teach men how to correct and hide imperfections (100€). The boutique is located at 176, boulevard Saint-Germain, in Paris's 6th arrondissement (01 45 48 02 55).

Makeup

VISÉART

58, rue Charlot, 3rd arr.

✆ 09 64 03 23 19

Métro: Filles-du-Calvaire

Tuesday to Saturday 11 am to 7 pm

www.viseart.com (E)

Viséart, a cosmetic line created by a French artist and stylist, is well known to professional makeup artists in the fashion and entertainment industries. It sells to the public from its boutique in the northern end of the Marais district. The boutique has a modern, cheerful candy-shop vibe, and features a makeup bar where clients can have their makeup done and learn tricks from experts. Customers are encouraged to experiment and play with Viséart's products. The staff is friendly, proficient in English, and passionate about makeup, and Viséart makes for an amusing and informative stop along a Marais shopping itinerary.

Viséart is known primarily for its foundations, and prides itself on the light feeling and smooth texture of its products. Its bases and powders are silicone-free and made with microencapsulated powders and pigments. The product that put Viséart on the map is its Teint Lissant, a cream foundation in a compact. It comes in fourteen colors, but the pros in the shop like to mix and blend to create the perfect match for a customer's skin (31.50€).

The boutique offers a full range of cosmetics, nail polish, and a few skincare products used to prepare the skin for makeup application. The Palette 12 Correcteur, a camouflage concealer and foundation palette, is a popular product; it contains twelve cream colors that multitask as concealers, neutralizers, contours, blushes, and foundations (45€). Viséart products are also sold in New York and in Cologne, Germany, and with limited availability online—but for a selection of more than fifty lipsticks and sixty eye shadows, shoppers must stop into the Paris boutique.

MAQUILLAGE CAFFÈ

8, rue Nicolas Flamel, 4th arr.

☎ 01 48 04 02 94

Métro: Hôtel de Ville

Tuesday, Wednesday, Saturday, Sunday 11 am to 8 pm,
Thursday and Friday 11 am to 9 pm,
but hours vary by season; consult website

www.couleur-caramel.com/maquillage-caffe.html (E)

"Ethical cosmetics" is the tagline of Maquillage Caffè, two boutiques opened by the French natural cosmetic brand Couleur Caramel. The shops are designed as a playful and interactive space where clients come to touch, try, and create their own makeup palettes from more than five hundred cosmetics. All of Maquillage Caffè's products are made from 100% natural ingredients. The eye shadow comes in a wide range of colors and is one of the brand's best-selling products (10.50€).

The boutique is divided into two spaces, the Color Bar and the Lounge Space. The bar is made up of several makeup stations, including one especially for children. The lounge is a place to sink back into comfy couches and enjoy a cup of tea. If testing cosmetics with a lot of other people sounds as unsavory as buying food from the bulk bins at the grocery store, you may find comfort in the fact that each person is required to wash up before trying anything. This hygiene policy is strictly enforced.

Maquillage Caffè offers workshops and special classes. The Special Brunch from 11 am to 2 pm on Sundays is a twenty-minute makeup class and application (16€). The Girlfriends Workshop can be booked for two to eight people who want to learn about makeup together (40€, 1½ hours). The shop also offers services for special occasions, including bridal makeup (90€, includes trial) and Halloween and Mardi Gras (12€, 15 minutes).

Maquillage Caffè is ethically and environmentally-minded. Makeup packaging is made from recycled materials, and the boutique itself tried to use recycled materials in its space and design. The chairs are made from recycled industrial drums, industrial ink cartridges were used for light fittings, and the wood-cutting system used during the building phase recycled its scraps for use in other products. The company's immediate goal is to have all of its formulas certified by Ecocert—an official French designation that certifies the amount and origins of natural or organic ingredients in a product.

Alternate Location:

10, rue Jean Du Bellay, 4th arr.

✆ 01 40 46 05 74

BY TERRY

30, rue de la Trémoille, 8th arr.

✆ 01 44 43 04 04

Métro: Franklin-D.-Roosevelt or George V

Monday to Saturday 10:30 am to 7 pm

www.byterry.com (E)

A brief detour on her educational path brought Terry de Gunzburg to the world of beauty: before entering Paris's School of Fine Arts she decided to take a makeup course taught by the famed Carita sisters. When *Vogue* needed a makeup artist for a fashion shoot and no one else was available, Maria Carita sent de Gunzburg. That day changed her life's direction—she quickly developed an international reputation as a makeup artist. Her style was characterized by its natural look; de Gunzburg offered bright and youthful-looking skin to women of all ages. She spent two decades working with the Carita sisters and Yves Saint Laurent, and in the late 1990s left to develop and advocate her own concept.

Terry de Gunzburg launched her cosmetic line based on the principles of fashion. She wanted to move away from standardization and towards made-to-measure luxury products. There are three lines in her collection. Haute Couleur is an exclusive service available only at the Véro-Dodat location in Paris, where personalized cosmetics are created for clients. The Couture line is created in limited quantities using expensive and high-performing ingredients, and the Prêt-à-Porter range meets the needs of a broader range of clients, with more modest prices.

One of her most dynamic products is the Éclat Opulent Soin de

Teint Nutri Liftant, a foundation created for mature skin. It uses hyaluronic acid to fill in wrinkles and an optical corrector to conceal signs of aging and fatigue (98€, 30ml). By Terry is also known for its ultrafine eye shadow, Ombre Soyuese, which comes in colors like Coffee Bean and Dappled Bronze (29€).

Makeup classes and services are offered by appointment in the By Terry boutiques. Guests can reserve a session for day or evening makeup application (110€, 1 hour), a private lesson (165€, 1½ hours), or bridal makeup (210€). The staff is friendly and proficient in English. Each of the boutiques has a specialty: the laboratory on Véro-Dodat creates the Haute Couleur products, and the Glowing Room at the Victor Hugo boutique offers skincare and facial treatments.

By Terry has department-store counters in Paris inside Galeries Lafayette in the 9th arrondissement, Le Bon Marché, and in Printemps Haussmann. The brand is sold in the U.S. at Barneys department stores and through the By Terry website.

Alternate Locations:

21, passage Véro-Dodat, 1st arr.
✆ 01 44 76 00 76

36, passage Véro-Dodat, 1st arr.
✆ 01 44 76 00 76

10, avenue Victor Hugo , 16th arr.
✆ 01 55 73 00 73

MAKE UP FOR EVER

5, rue de La Boétie, 8th arr.

☎ 01 53 05 93 30

Métro: Saint-Augustin or Miromesnil

Monday to Saturday 10:30 am to 7 pm

www.makeupforever.com (E)

:::

I n 1984, Dany Sanz, a French painter and sculptor turned makeup artist, founded Make Up For Ever to create products for the fashion and entertainment industries. As Sanz gained notoriety, she opened a boutique in Paris's 8th arrondissement where professional makeup artists could find exclusive products. In 2002, she opened an academy in Paris and welcomed students from all over the world.

Sanz's style ranges from the classic to the avant-garde. The cosmetic line boasts over fourteen hundred products, including more than 125 eyeshadows and ninety shades of lipstick. Specialized products are available to meet the needs of theater and performing arts groups, as well as the fashion industry. The experts at Make Up For Ever's exclusive shop on La Boétie are energetic and anxious to help clients. In addition to cosmetics, the shop also sells makeup tools and accessories. Make Up For Ever products are available internationally in about twenty professional boutiques, and in the U.S. at Sephora.

The Sephora store on the Champs-Elysées hosts the Make Up For Ever Make up School, where anyone with twenty minutes can have their makeup applied or learn the basics from a professional. The kiosk offers Smoky Eyes, Faux Cils Naturels (natural-looking false eyelash application), and Teint HD Zéro Défauts, or "flawless foundation" (25€ per lesson). The Total Look lessons last one hour and include Maquillage Jour (daytime makeup), Maquillage Soir (evening makeup), and Tendance, or trendy looks (60€). The school is open every day from 11 am to 11 pm. Sessions can be reserved by calling 01 45 61 19 25.

NOCIBÉ

187, rue Saint-Honoré, 1st arr.

✆ 01 40 15 91 73

Métro: Pyramides, Tuileries, or Palais-Royal

Monday to Saturday 10 am to 7 pm

www.nocibe.fr

Nocibé is one of the largest cosmetic and perfume chains in France, with over four hundred locations. There are a handful of boutiques in each arrondissement. The stores are bright and the staff is generally knowledgeable, but with hit-or-miss English. The boutiques sell a huge range of perfume, makeup, and skincare collections. Nocibé carries the big makeup brands like Chanel, Christian Dior, and Lancôme, as well as lower-priced lines like Bourjois (the parent company of Chanel). It features skincare products from companies like Clarins, Clinique, and Decléor.

The location on Rue de Rivoli, near the St. Paul métro station, has a salon and *parapharmacie* upstairs. Salon services are efficient and pleasant; this location offers facials, massages, body wraps, cellulite treatments, waxing, makeup, and nail services. The *institut* offers a surprising variety of spa treatments, including a marine-based facial, Le Soin Bienfait Marin (55€, 75 minutes); a hydrating, anti-aging facial, Le Soin Anti-Temps au Collagène (56€, 75 minutes); and a facial designed especially for teenagers, Le Soin Pur Ado (32€, 35 minutes). Nocibé is a good option for a last-minute manicure (25€ with polish) or pedicure (31€, 45 minutes). The salespeople are generous with samples once you are checking out, so be sure to ask.

YVES ROCHER

Centre de Beauté Yves Rocher
68, rue de Rennes, 6th arr.
✆ 01 40 49 08 98
Métro: Saint-Sulpice
Monday 11 am to 7 pm, Tuesday to Saturday 10 am to 7 pm
www.yvesrocherusa.com (E)

::

The Yves Rocher brand has made its way around the world, with likeable French plant-based skincare products and cosmetics at reasonable to moderate prices. The chain differs from Marionnaud and Nocibé in that it is limited to its own collections. Yves Rocher has a number of products that are Parisian bestsellers: the Gommage Gourmand aux Noyaux d'Abricot, a creamy facial scrub with a fruity scent that uses apricot stones to help exfoliate (6.50€, 50ml); the Baume Hydratant-Baume Nature, a hydrating lip balm made with grape extracts (3.90€, 4g); and the 2 en 1 Beauté et Jeunesse-Arnica Essentiel, a protective hand cream made with arnica (4.50€, 75ml).

Several boutiques have salons that provide quality treatments in an efficient environment. Facials, massages, and exfoliations, as well as makeup application, pedicures, manicures, and hair removal are available. A revitalizing facial that uses vegetable extracts (50€, 75 minutes) and the Grand Soin des Pieds, a complete pedicure, are two favorites (50€ + 12€ for polish, 45 minutes).

MARIONNAUD

104, avenue des Champs-Elysées, 8th arr.
✆ 01 53 96 50 00
Métro: George V or Charles-de-Gaulle-Étoile
Monday to Sunday 10 am to midnight
www.marionnaud.fr

It is no exaggeration to say that there is a Marionnaud on practically every corner in Paris. With hundreds of convenient locations, Marionnaud is a favorite among Parisians in need of quality beauty services at affordable prices. Each location is different—some sell perfume and makeup, while others have a salon upstairs, which is indicated by the word *institut* on the window or sign.

The ground floor of Marionnaud is a perfume shop that carries the industry's big names: Lolita Lempicka, Kenzo, Hermès, and Guerlain, to name a few. The boutiques sell a wide assortment of skincare, makeup, and nail care products. They also have a section for men's skincare and beauty needs. The salon offers makeup, nail, and waxing services, as well as facials using Decléor products, massage, exfoliation treatments, and tanning services. Daytime and evening makeup application are some of the most popular services (19€ and 32€). An aromatherapy massage at Marionnaud lacks the ambience of one done at a spa, but is reasonably priced and easily reserved (60€, 1 hour).

Perfume

L'ARTISAN PARFUMEUR
2, rue de l'Amiral de Coligny, 1st arr.
☎ 01 44 88 27 50
Métro: Louvre-Rivoli
Monday to Saturday 10 am to 7 pm
www.artisanparfumeur.com (E)

L'Artisan Parfumeur has created a novel concept with its deliciously scented boutique in the 1st arrondissement. The ground floor is a space for clients to discover, smell, and test all of L'Artisan's fragrances. Upstairs, perfume workshops are offered for novices. There is a tasting bar where guests can acquaint themselves with some of the flowers that go into the scents. For a memorable experience, L'Artisan Parfumeur will cre-

ate a one-of-a-kind perfume or cologne that speaks to your individual desires. The concept behind the brand is to provoke visceral memories through scent—whether it is the recollection of a season, a home, a travel experience, an event, or a person.

The staff is patient and knowledgeable; many speak English very well, and all are willing to take the time to baby-step clients through each of the fragrances. The brand was created in 1976 and was first known for its home fragrances. Two years later, the company released a perfume, Mûre et Musc, with hints of musk and notes of blackberry—it remains a bestseller today. L'Artisan Parfumeur makes scented candles and uniquely decorative scent-diffusing amber balls for the home.

The octagonally-shaped perfume bottles are simple and elegant in design, with a narrow, rectangular label that varies in color with each perfume. The perfumes are categorized as either floral or spicy; the spicy collection is unisex, while the florals are intended for women. L'Artisan Parfumeur is well known for a scent that captures the essence of summer, Premier Figuier. Most recently, the brand has launched an organic line, called Jatamansi, made from essential oils and all-natural ingredients. Jatamansi is taken from the Sanskrit name for *le nard de l'Himalaya*, a small flower found in the Asian mountain range. *Eau de toilette* bottles are priced at 65€ for 50ml and 90€ for 100ml, although some of the limited-edition fragrances are more expensive. Products are available at authorized boutiques throughout the world and online.

Alternate Locations:

99, rue de Rivoli, 1st arr.
✆ 01 42 96 21 44

34, rue des Francs-Bourgeois, 3rd arr.
✆ 01 42 77 80 28

32, rue du Bourg-Tibourg, 4th arr.
✆ 01 48 04 55 66

24, boulevard Raspail, 7th arr.
✆ 01 42 22 23 32

ÉTAT LIBRE D'ORANGE

69, rue des Archives, 3rd arr.

✆ 01 42 78 30 09

Métro: Arts et Métiers or Temple

Tuesday to Saturday noon to 7:30 pm

www.etatlibredorange.com (E)

Anarchy in a bottle? With a label that reads, "*Le parfum est mort, vive le parfum!*" ("Perfume is dead, long live perfume!"), État Libre d'Orange is, at the very least, avant-garde. With a collection that includes anti-establishment classics like Jasmin et Cigarette, Putain des Palaces (Hotel Slut), Encens & Bubblegum (Incense & Bubblegum), and Sécrétions Magnifiques, État Libre's director Etienne De Swardt has declared his independence from the classic world of perfume. De Swardt spent seven years at Givenchy before he left to create "Oh My Dog!" a fragrance for canines. Now he has created a niche perfume house, with "noses" who are encouraged to create without regard for market research or commercial viability.

Jasmin et Cigarette is simple yet seductive, with scents of jasmine, tobacco, apricot, and amber. It recalls the era of glamorous Hollywood starlets and contemporary *provocateuses*, who, with cigarette in hand, seduce men and entrance the public. Putain des Palaces uses hints of rose, violet, leather, ginger, and mandarin orange to encourage women to "liberate their own fantasies of seduction." From packaging to perfumes, this is a brand with a sense of humor that pokes fun at traditional ideas of what a perfume should be (most fragrances 59€, 50ml). État Libre d'Orange also creates scented candles for the home. Products are available at its Paris boutique, from authorized retailers internationally, and online.

CANZI

2-4, rue Ferdinand Duval, 4th arr.
☎ 01 42 78 09 37
Métro: Saint-Paul
Tuesday to Sunday 11 am to 8 pm, Monday 6 pm to 8 pm

Canzi is a cutting-edge *biocosmétique* shop, with a collection of products that are 100% organic and 100% natural. You may well find the brand's creator and "nose," Stéphane Mottay, behind the counter dispensing advice *sur mesure* (tailored to a client's tastes). In his Marais space, Mottay holds weekly workshops to demystify the fabrication of natural cosmetics and skincare during which he teaches students how to mix their own perfumes and skincare products. The workshops are in French, but Stéphane is fluent in English. It was while living in the United States that Mottay developed simple procedures that led to the creation of his own product line. The shop is modern, refined, and simple, as is the Canzi collection.

His bestsellers include a soothing balm made from shea butter, argan oil, and jasmine (30€), and a remarkable exfoliant made from Loire-Atlantique sea salt that is steeped in a blend of citrus. Mottay has hand-selected well-being products from other natural brands, among them Weleda, Alma Carmel, Phyt's, and Dr. Hauschka. Mottay's handmade soaps, sold by the slice, are scented with cinnamon-vanilla, ginger-ginseng, and orange flower (5€). The Canzi line includes perfume, face and body creams, and oils. Mottay's Parfum Oriental is a scent made with vetiver, vanilla, and orange flower (7€, 50ml). This boutique is the place to find and create one-of-a-kind *cosmé-souvenirs* from Paris.

THE DIFFERENT COMPANY

10, rue Ferdinand Duval, 4th arr.

✆ 01 42 78 19 34

Métro: Saint-Paul

Tuesday to Saturday noon to 7:30 pm

www.thedifferentcompany.com (E)

::

This sleek, light-filled, modern shop in the 4th arrondissement is home to a remarkable concept, co-created in 2000 by famed perfumer Jean-Claude Ellena and luxury designer Thierry de Baschmakoff. Ellena has since left to work as the exclusive perfumer at Hermès, but his daughter Céline continues the family tradition and has created perfumes for The Different Company since her father's departure.

The company's philosophy was a rejection of mass production and the use of chemicals in the perfume world. The founders felt that modern fragrances were devoid of creativity and were being developed in response to market research. In short, they wanted a return to the traditional values of French perfumeries. There are no synthetics or chemicals in any of the fragrances; it is one of the few companies to be approved by Greenpeace's Cosmetox guide, a study that investigates the level of toxicity in cosmetics.

Today, The Different Company offers eleven perfumes; Oriental Lounge is the newest. Clients first sniff fragrances from wine glasses; the shape of the glass allows the scent to breathe and release its full complexity. Each scent is sold in a refillable bottle (*flacon rechargeable*) made of heavy glass, designed to be an art object in itself. Sublime Balkiss, named after the Queen of Sheba, is one of the company's most popular fragrances, with notes of blueberries, blackberries, patchouli, and Damascus rose from Bulgaria. Inspired by Jean-Claude Ellena's trip to China, Osmanthus was created from the smallest flower in the world, the osthmanthus—forty-four pounds of flowers are required to create 250ml of Osmanthus. The fragrance has notes of the tiny flower, along with bergamot, orange, rose, and musk (82€, 50ml; 129€, 90ml; refills 74€, 50ml).

MARIE ANTOINETTE

5, rue d'Ormesson, 4th arr.
✆ 01 42 71 25 07
Métro: Saint-Paul
Tuesday to Sunday noon to 8 pm
www.marieantoinetteparis.fr

M arie Antoinette is the kind of boutique you dream of accidentally discovering as you wander the streets of Paris—a tiny, treasure-filled shop that feels like a real "find." Just blocks from La Place des Vosges is one of the most charming squares in Paris—unknown to many Parisians—La Place du Marché Sainte Catherine. Marie Antoinette's storefront on the place is shiny and red, with the words *"parfums et senteurs d'exception"* (exceptional perfumes and scents) inscribed across the glass. The shop's name at first glance seems to refer to the queen of France, who adored perfume (especially the fragrance of roses), but the full meaning behind the name is more personal. The shop's delightful owner, Antonio De Figueiredo, is more than happy to explain to his guests the inspiration, as well as the history, behind each carefully selected product in his shop.

De Figueiredo loves all things olfactory and chose this quiet place to showcase a trove of scents from niche brands, including a huge selection of products from the Portuguese company Claus Porto. (De Figueiredo has a fondness for Claus Porto, as some of his best memories are from the time spent with his Portuguese grandmother.) The candles—made from a soy-based wax, without artificial colors or preservatives—each burn for seventy hours and come in charming, beautifully designed boxes. The eighteen different fragrances are derived from essential oils. There are also home fragrances and luxurious soaps in scents such as Orange Amber, Red Poppy, Mimosa, and Grapefruit Fig, wrapped in vintage-looking paper.

De Figueiredo chooses boutique brands such as P. Frapin & Cie and Mad et Len, and one made exclusively for De Figueiredo's boutique that must be ordered two months in advance (65€). The fragrance is alcohol-free and handmade using natural essences. He also offers lovely bath salts (8.50€) and intoxicatingly fragrant room sprays (12.50€).

SENTEURS DE FÉE

10, rue de Sévigné, 4th arr.

✆ 01 44 54 97 27

Métro: Saint-Paul

Sunday and Monday 2 pm to 7:30 pm, Tuesday to Thursday
11 am to 7:30 pm, Friday and Saturday noon to 8 pm

This little shop in the Marais with a vintage ambience is the creation of aromatherapy and cosmetics expert Katia Bielli. It has an apothecary-like feel to it, and the products that Bielli creates are almost entirely natural and made from essential oils. The founder and her assistants are informative and attentive. The boutique features scented candles, bath oils, home fragrances, skincare products, and perfumes.

The boutique's bestseller, Le Nectar de Rose, made with macadamia nuts, apricot stones, and rose essential oil, is a hydrating cream that calms and nourishes (40€). Senteurs de Fée offers nine perfumes, including a delightful rose scent (70€). Lighter fragrances are available in the Eau Parfumée collection. Pretty, feminine gold-clad bottles contain fresh scents of ylang-ylang, orange flowers, and geranium. The bath salts are a must-try, made from sea salt harvested in the Guérande region and soaked in essential oils. Choose from mixtures that provide a relaxing, detoxifying, or energizing effect (12€, 600g).

DIPTYQUE

34, boulevard Saint-Germain, 5th arr.

✆ 01 43 26 77 44

Métro: Maubert-Mutualité

Monday to Saturday 10 am to 7 pm

www.diptyqueparis.com (E)

hree friends, inspired by nature and travel and motivated by the same creative passion, teamed up in 1961 to create Diptyque. The first shop was a chic bazaar filled with textiles and fabrics designed by the owners, as well as goods brought back from their travels. In 1963, this group—an interior decorator, a painter, and a set designer—released three scented candles: Aubépine, Cannelle, and Thé (hawthorn, cinnamon, and tea).

In 1968, Diptyque launched its first eau de toilette, L'Eau. The fragrance is an infusion of spices and flowers, containing cinnamon, clove, geranium, sandalwood, and rose; the scent was resurrected from a sixteenth-century potpourri and clove pomander recipe (50€, 50ml). Inspired by their fine-arts backgrounds, the trio designed the brand's now-iconic oval-shaped label with black lettering. The perfume labels are simple and clean and evoke a sense of the vintage, recalling pastoral scenes from antiquity.

Candles come in floral (Gardenia, Rose Geranium, Mexican Orange Blossom); fruity (Fig Tree, Berries, Oyédo); herbal (Fresh Mown Hay, Wild Fennel, Green Mint); woody (Woodfire, Cypress, Myrrh); and spicy (Pomander, Musk, Cinnamon) varieties (35€). Diptyque also reinvented a nineteenth-century astringent recipe, Vinaigre de Toilette, which can be used as a soothing aftershave, bath oil, or rinse that adds shine to hair (33€, 100ml). The boutiques carry room fragrances, body creams, lotion, oil, and shower gel in Diptyque's signature scents.

Alternate Locations:

8, rue des Francs Bourgeois, 3rd arr.
✆ 01 48 04 95 57

IN PRINTEMPS DE LA BEAUTÉ
64, boulevard Haussman, 9th arr.
✆ 01 42 82 41 01

DETAILLE

10, rue Saint-Lazare, 9th arr.

☎ 01 48 78 68 50

Métro: Notre-Dame-de-Lorette

Tuesday to Saturday 11 am to 2 pm, 3 pm to 7 pm

www.detaille.com (E)

A step into Detaille is a trip back in time—this authentic little boutique, Detaille's original shop, opened in 1905. The Countess de Presle herself opened and managed this location. The Countess was one of the first people in France to own an automobile, which did not have a windshield; she quickly noticed the dehydrating effect the wind and elements had on her face. She teamed up with a chemist friend, Marcellin Berthelot, and created the moisturizing lotion Baume Automobile, which continues to be a bestseller for the shop. Made with zinc oxide, minerals, and wheat proteins, it softens and protects the skin (55€, 65ml).

As the Countess's skincare line developed, so did her list of clients. The Queen of Bulgaria, the Queen of Belgium, and several maharajahs and princesses were among her loyal aristocratic clientele. Detaille has survived all of these years with simple and efficient products. The modern line of skincare combines plant and essential oils with floral waters.

Detaille sells five *eaux de toilette* for men. Par 4 is a seductive cologne, with notes of vetiver, bergamot, white thyme, and basil. Aéroplane is Detaille's top seller, with its fresh, citrusy scent of lemon, bergamot, basil, and mint. There are also five fragrances for women. The classic powdered perfume, 1905, has touches of violet, blackcurrant, jasmine, ylang-ylang, and rose. The superb Dolcia is a subtle blend of peach and lemon tree flowers, cinnamon with notes of wood, osthmanthus, and amber (all 85€, 100ml).

ARTISAN NATURE

123, rue Saint-Maur, 11th arr.

☎ 01 43 38 50 03

Métro: Parmentier

Tuesday to Saturday 2 pm to 7:30 pm

www.artisannature.fr

Artisan Nature is a collaboration between Jean-Charles Sommerard and two friends, Patrice Amblard and Philippe Bohin, ambassadors for the hip side of the organic movement and believers in its compatibility with a modern lifestyle. The brightly colored boutique sells artisan-made, certified 100% organic products. Artisan Nature is also the first floral water bar in Paris: Sommerard whips up fresh fruit drinks accented with essen-

tial oils and floral waters at the bar along the back of the shop. The drinks are perfectly seasonal, fresh, and remarkably delicious. You may be mystified for a moment as you try to deconstruct these *aromadrinks* and *floradrinks*, which are often topped with edible flowers. The Fémina is made from apple and mango juice, orange essential oil, and rose floral water (6€).

The boutique is packed with handmade, top-quality products. Patrice Amblard is a third generation apiculturist. His honey products are produced in a way that respects the bees and the ecosystems that surround them. Philippe Bohin is a holistic stylist who develops natural hair care and coloring products made from henna, vegetable and essential oils, and walnut husks. Together the group's motto is "*Beaux, Jeunes et terriblement Bios*" ("Handsome, Young and Frighteningly Organic").

After a forty-five-minute consultation with Sommerard, during which he observes the client's personality, he creates a perfume *sur mesure* based on the known properties of each of the thirty-three essential oils available in his boutique. The result is a creation that reflects the memories, hopes, and passions of the client (50€–80€). He creates personalized shampoos and shower gels based on the same process. Artisan Nature also sells other handmade personal and skincare products, as well as *parfums de cuisine*, Sommerard's personal blends of essential oils that complement cuisine.

SEVESSENCE

28, rue de la Fontaine au Roi, 11th arr.

☎ 01 47 00 32 29

Métro: Parmentier

Open by appointment

www.sevessence.com

Jean-Charles Sommerard's irrepressible passion for the therapeutic properties of essential oils is difficult to resist; after spending a few minutes with him, any skeptic will probably be converted into a believer. His micro-boutique, located in an up-and-coming area of the 11th arrondissement, is filled with 100% certified organic essential oils, vegetable oils, and floral waters made with ingredients harvested from his family's fields in

Provence and Madagascar.

Sommerard's father and grandfather were pioneers in the field of growing and distilling organic essential oils. Michel Sommerard, his father, founded Flôrame, one of the first companies on the market to harvest, distill, and distribute them. The cinnamon, eucalyptus, and ylang-ylang at Sevessence are all grown on his father's plantation in Madagascar (5€–20€, 10ml). Jean-Charles, who co-created Artisan Nature and divides his time between the two shops, creates individualized perfumes (50€–80€, 30ml) and shares his knowledge of essential oils through workshops and city-wide events. Most recently, Sommerard blended fragrances *sur mesure* for guests at a Christian Dior haute couture event. He also collaborated with the Hôtel Crillon on Place de la Concorde to create an olfactory signature for the luxury palace.

BEAUTY SECRETS REVEALED

Best Products From the Pharmacie

Fancy boutiques or department stores aren't the only places to find some of the best cosmetic and skincare products on the French market. French women are discreet about their beauty routines, but it is no secret that they find many of their favorite products in their local *pharmacies*. The *pharmacie* is akin in some ways to the American drugstore: inside, you can pick up a prescription ordered by a doctor, but you can also find over-the-counter remedies that in the U.S. would be available by prescription only. The pharmacists on staff are trained professionals who offer healthcare advice as well as product recommendations. *Parapharmacies* sell the same products as *pharmacies*, but do not dispense medical advice or prescriptions.

Shopping for skincare products at the *pharmacie* is almost a rite of passage for young French girls. Celine Helmstetter, the spa director at Anne Sémonin, fondly recalls her transition to *pharmacie* products. French mothers, Helmstetter explains, teach their daughters at an early age to establish a skincare routine by maintaining a balanced diet, washing their faces daily with a simple cleanser or makeup remover, and, depending on skin type, using a light hydrating cream. By the time the girls become adolescents, they may be facing more complicated skin issues—many of them visit the *pharmacie* for professional advice and add a *sérum*, a targeted treatment for specific skin issues, to their routine.

The following is a list of must-haves from the *pharmacie*; fortunately, some of them are available in the U.S. and online. Avène and Nuxe are well represented among these "secrets"; both brands have a mass popular and critical following.

Daily Moisturizer: Avène Hydrance Optimale Légère UV SPF20 Anti-Oxydant (18.50€, 40ml) A light daily moisturizer for all skin types that includes UV protection and anti-oxidant properties.

Day or Night Cream: Nuxe Crème Fraîche de Beauté Formule "Light" (26€, 50ml) A moisturizing cream for combination skin, characterized by an oily T-zone and dry cheeks. Men love this product.

Day or Night Cream: Crème Fraîche de Beauté Suractivée (29€, 60ml) A more intense moisturizer than the "light" formula, designed for skin in need of added hydration. It is made with eight plant milks, five plant saps, essential oils, and pomegranate.

Toner: Caudalie Eau de Beauté (10€, 30ml) This toning spray was inspired by the "elixir of youth" used by Queen Isabelle of Hungary. It is made with grape extracts and essential oil of rosemary, orange blossom, and rose extracts. It also works well as an aftershave for men.

Body Lotion: Bioderma Atoderm Crème (19€, 500ml) An all-over body moisturizer that is gentle enough for the entire family. Its texture is thick, and it does not irritate reactive or sensitive skin.

Treatment Cream: Avène Cicalfate Crème Réparatrice Antibactérienne (7.6€, 40ml) A cream used to treat skin irritations, like dry or blotchy patches; it is also recommended for use after minor dermatological procedures. Avène products are made with water from its thermal sources, or hot springs.

General Skincare: Nuxe Huile Prodigieuse Soin Multi-fonctions (25€, 100ml) A bestseller for Nuxe, made with borage, St. John's wort, sweet almond, camellia, hazelnut, and macadamia oils. The oil can be used on skin and hair; a few drops make for a relaxing bath.

Cleanser and Makeup Remover: Bioderma Créaline H2O Sans Parfum (10.5€, 250ml) A gentle and effective daily cleanser and makeup remover, Créaline H2O is a favorite with Parisians of all ages and walks of life. It is a micellar solution targeted to sensitive skin, but good for all types. Créaline can be bought sans *parfum* (fragrance-free) or *parfumée* (with fragrance).

Lip Balm: Nuxe Rêve de Miel Baume Lèvres (11€,15 ml) This lip balm is a mainstay in Parisian purses and pockets; it soothes lips with acacia honey and shea butter.

Body Spray: Avène Eau Thermale (7.5€, 300ml) Body spray that doubles as a post-sun or post-waxing treatment.

Eye Area Cream: Nuxe Contour des Yeux Prodigieux (17.5€, 15ml) Anti-aging cream made with green tea and floral waters.

Acne Treatment: Vichy Normaderm Soin Hydratant Anti-Imperfections (15.5€, 50ml) Anti-acne moisturizer made with Zincadone A, salicylic acid, and Vichy thermal waters. This product won the 2009 Vichy User's Choice Award.

Facial Scrub: Cattier Gommage à l'Argile Blanche (5€, 100ml) A facial exfoliant with aloe vera and white clay that comes from Montmorillon, France. It carries the Cosmébio label, issued by Ecocert, which designates a certified organic cosmetic product.

Anti-Cellulite: Weleda Huile de Massage Minceur (23€, 100ml) This entirely natural massage oil is made to reduce cellulite. It is formulated with silver birch leaves, rosemary, and holly.

Hand Cream: Nuxe Rêve de Miel Crème Mains et Ongles (11€, 75ml) Sweet almond, Chilean rose, and avocado oils, along with acacia honey, are ingredients of this nourishing hand cream.

BEAUTY ON THE FLY

If time does not permit a visit to a proper spa while in Paris, both of Paris's major airports (Charles de Gaulle and Orly) offer well-being services for people on the go. Appointments can be booked, but walk-ins are also welcome. Travelers can treat themselves to facials, massages, nail services, and more before they take to the skies.

BE RELAX

Reservations: check website for closest location within
airport terminals, and call appropriate number
www.berelax.com

Be Relax has seven locations for massage and well-being treatments throughout Charles de Gaulle Terminals 1 and 2, as well as branches in Orly Sud and Orly Ouest. Be Relax offers three chair massages: Be Up, a revitalizing deep massage designed to reduce fatigue and stress (31€, 20 minutes); Be Relax, a massage designed to help travelers relax before a long flight (41€, 30 minutes); and Be, a soothing foot massage based on reflexology techniques (45€, 30 minutes). There are express and classic pedicure and manicure services, as well as oxygen and aromatherapy add-ons (18€–46€). More comprehensive spa services, including table massage and waxing, are available at the location in Terminal S3 (a satellite of Terminal 2, accessible from 2E). There are also a number of freestanding auto-massage chairs in various locations throughout the Charles de Gaulle terminal.

MEN'S LOUNGE
Terminal 2D, Charles de Gaulle airport
No phone number available

More than 64% of travelers that come through Paris's airports are men, and Men's Lounge is dedicated to their well-being. Located in Terminal 2D of Charles de Gaulle, the sleek boutique sells cologne as well as men's skincare and hair products. Spa by Nickel is located inside the boutique, offering express facial, hand, and body treatments (15€–40€). The store is also home to the "Skincare Bar," an interactive software program that helps men understand their skin types and individual needs, and offers product and skincare recommendations. Men's Lounge is a convenient stop for jet-lagged businessmen and tired travelers.

INSTITUT GUERLAIN
✆ 01 49 75 49 31

This mini-salon in Orly Ouest offers abbreviated treatments for exhausted travelers or those in need of a quick beauty pick-me-up. It is located inside the Beauty Unlimited boutique.

Index

ABOUT THE AUTHOR

Kim Horton Levesque has worked as a writer and French translator in the U.S. beauty industry for the past three years. She has a background in teaching and journalism and is now focusing on travel writing. Kim spent many years studying and working in France and Western Europe and continues to be an avid traveler. She lives in Phoenix, Arizona, with her husband and three daughters.

ABOUT THE PHOTOGRAPHER

Kristyn Moore is a photographer who specializes in interiors, architecture, still life, and natural light portraiture. She was interested in photography from a young age, and developed her style while living in Europe. Her work can be seen at www.kristyn-moore.com

OTHER BOOKS ABOUT PARIS AND FRANCE
FROM THE LITTLE BOOKROOM

To see complete information, log on to www.littlebookroom.com or email (editorial@littlebookroom.com) or call us for a catalog (646-215-2500).

EATING AND DRINKING
The Pâtisseries of Paris by Jamie Cahill
The Best Wine Bars & Shops in Paris by Pierrick Jégu
The Brasseries of Paris by François Thomazeau
The Authentic Bistros of Paris by François Thomazeau
The Historic Restaurants of Paris by Ellen Williams
Food Wine Burgundy by David Downie
Pudlo France 2008-2009 by Gilles Pudlowski
Pudlo Normandy & Brittany by Gilles Pudlowski
Pudlo Alsace by Gilles Pudlowski
Pudlo Provence, the Cote d'Azur & Monaco by Gilles Pudlowski

CULTURE
Paris and her Remarkable Women: A Guide by Lorraine Liscio
Quiet Corners of Paris by Jean-Christophe Napias
Paris Quiz by Dominique Lesbros
Literary Paris: A Guide by Jessica Powell
The Impressionists' Paris by Ellen Williams
Picasso's Paris by Ellen Williams
Walks Through Napoleon & Josephine's Paris by Diana Reid Haig

SHOPPING
Paris: Made by Hand by Pia Jane Bijkerk
Markets of Paris by Dixon and Ruthanne Long
The Best Vintage, Antique and Collectible Shops in Paris by Edith Pauly
Chic Shopping Paris by Rebecca Perry Magniant
Paris Chic & Trendy by Adrienne Ribes-Tiphaine
The Flea Markets of France by Sandy Price

ACCOMMODATIONS
Boutique and Chic Hotels in Paris by Lionel Paillès